NEW DIRECTIONS FOR ADULT AND CONTINUING EDUCATION

Susan Imel, *Ohio State University*
EDITOR-IN-CHIEF

W9-DCY-639

Team Teaching and Learning in Adult Education

Mary-Jane Eisen
University of Hartford

Elizabeth J. Tisdell
National Louis University

EDITORS

Number 87, Fall 2000

JOSSEY-BASS
San Francisco

TEAM TEACHING AND LEARNING IN ADULT EDUCATION
Mary-Jane Eisen, Elizabeth J. Tisdell (eds.)
New Directions for Adult and Continuing Education, no. 87
Susan Imel, Editor-in-Chief

Microfilm copies of issues and articles are available in 16mm and 35mm, as well as microfiche in 105mm, through University Microfilms Inc., 300 North Zeeb Road, Ann Arbor, Michigan 48106-1346.

ISSN 1052-2891   ISBN 0-7879-5425-X

NEW DIRECTIONS FOR ADULT AND CONTINUING EDUCATION is part of The Jossey-Bass Higher and Adult Education Series and is published quarterly by Jossey-Bass Inc., 350 Sansome Street, San Francisco, California 94104-1342. Periodicals postage paid at San Francisco, California, and at additional mailing offices. Postmaster: Send address changes to New Directions for Adult and Continuing Education, Jossey-Bass Inc., 350 Sansome Street, San Francisco, California 94104-1342.

SUBSCRIPTIONS cost $58.00 for individuals and $104.00 for institutions, agencies, and libraries.

EDITORIAL CORRESPONDENCE should be sent to the Editor-in-Chief, Susan Imel, ERIC/ACVE, 1900 Kenny Road, Columbus, Ohio 43210-1090. E-mail: imel.1@osu.edu.

Cover photograph by Wernher Krutein/PHOTOVAULT © 1990.

www.josseybass.com

Contents

EDITORS' NOTES

The field of adult and continuing education is a broad one indeed, with many different subdivisions, including adult development, aging, adult learning, workplace learning, and education for social transformation. Underpinning all of these, however, is an emphasis on teaching and learning. The purpose of this volume is twofold: to explore the dynamic and interrelational nature of team teaching and its potential to enhance both teaching and learning, and to offer new insights about how to incorporate it effectively in a variety of contexts.

Ironically, despite its seemingly low-tech nature relative to our high-tech times, team teaching is attracting greater attention than ever before. This is because it spotlights the learning side of the teaching-learning equation, an important new emphasis given the demands of the knowledge revolution to create and deliver new forms of knowledge continually. This shift in focus is also being fostered by an evolving vision of adult education in which ownership for both teaching and learning is shared in a variety of possible ways and contexts.

Teaming honors the multidirectionality of learning—the fact that no one person can be an expert on everything—and it also acknowledges that teachers can be learners and learners can be teachers. Team teachers and learners have the capacity to create new knowledge collaboratively—knowledge that is both embedded in and transcends their individual disciplines or life experiences.

Team teaching and learning is neither a direct result of past changes nor a complete departure from past practice. Rather, it is a reflection of the emerging emphasis on inclusivity. By this we mean the inclusion of different perspectives (disciplinary, cultural, and social and political, for example), of different methods (such as active learning, online education, and independent study), and of both teachers and learners in the multidirectional process of adult learning.

Furthermore, today's teachers are a new breed who continue to value their independence but do not wish to be isolated. They realize that there is much to be learned with and from colleagues. For instance, they can help each other develop the knowledge and skills to infuse learning with multidisciplinary and multicultural perspectives; educators can also support each other in keeping up with changes in information and technology that are transforming not only what is taught but also how it is delivered; and as more adults are accessing educational opportunities, teachers can help each other to address creatively the myriad demands of learners whose learning styles and learning objectives are increasingly diverse. At the same time, teaming provides a vibrant model of collaboration that learners can emulate and even participate in. It also fosters a sense of social connectedness and shared enthusiasm that is fortifying and renewing amid the escalating challenges and demands of teaching and learning today. So it is that the potential for improved teaching and professional development is enhanced.

In the chapters that follow, we share several variations on the theme of team teaching and learning. With the exception of the first chapter, all were coauthored and include snapshots of different applications of teaming in a number of unique educational contexts. To set the stage for viewing these diverse snapshots, one of us, Mary-Jane Eisen, develops a definition of team teaching and learning in Chapter One. She then provides an overview of many types of teaming arrangements by introducing two typologies, one based on team objectives and one based on team members' ways of working together.

In Chapters Two, Three, and Four, the authors discuss models of team teaching in higher education from both an administrative and a classroom perspective. In Chapter Two, Marcia Bundy Seabury and Karen Barrett give us insights from an administrative perspective into ways of creating and sustaining an undergraduate curriculum comprising over twenty team-taught, interdisciplinary courses. In Chapter Three, Candace Harris and Anne Harvey discuss how knowledge is co-created with teachers and students in a B.A. completion classroom of adult learners; they also show how their teaming enhances attention to diversity and facilitates dealing with controversial issues in the classroom. In Chapter Four, Gabriele Strohschen and Tom Heaney offer new insights into team teaching in an online graduate class in adult education. By using the metaphor of "This Isn't Kansas Anymore," they discuss how teaming helps negotiate both the realities of technology and democratic education in cyberspace. Although many of the pointers that these authors working in higher education share are most relevant for practitioners in similar contexts, their administrative and teaching strategies can certainly be applied in other settings as well.

The authors of Chapters Five and Six address ways that teaming to facilitate learning enhances both organizational learning and individual learning in very different settings. In the context of a recently deregulated public utility, Chapter Five's authors, Judy O'Neil and Sharon Lamm, introduce an action learning model that is gaining popularity in workplace settings across the country and internationally as well. Their snapshot includes a "double exposure" to two levels of teaming for learning. One involves learning coaches who guide teams of workers in managing major organizational change; the other involves the team of learning coaches who seek to unify their respective teams' efforts, while also helping each other become more professionally effective as action learning coaches. In Chapter Six, Todd Evans and Jane Hugo give a snapshot of a very different context, that of a national literacy organization, by discussing a decentralized team-based approach to training and certifying literacy volunteers. Local training teams meet the needs of the national organization, while allowing trainers and volunteers to have more control of their teaching and learning at the local level.

The authors of Chapters Seven and Eight focus their discussion and model of team teaching and learning on work in community-based settings, with particular attention to diversity and social change issues. Again, each pair of authors works in different settings. Viviana Aguilar and Ginlin Woo discuss working with American service volunteers on ways that they might attend to diversity issues in their own lives and in the communities in which they work. They highlight the importance of modeling cultural diversity within the training team and suggest ways of examining and challenging subtle attitudes and the manifestations of power relations based on gender, race, class, sexual orientation, and disability, with a view toward creating more equity. In Chapter Eight, Regina Curry and Phyllis Cunningham reconceptualize the notion of team teaching and learning in community-based contexts as co-learning and discuss how it operates in a community-based setting in Chicago's South Side. They contend that their concept of co-learning calls into question the notion of teacher as expert and learner as novice. Rather, co-learning equalizes power relations in the learning environment and sees all participants in the learning community as potential intellectuals and creators of knowledge.

Finally in the last chapter, as coeditors and coauthors, we discuss the process of editing this book as a team-teaching and -learning endeavor that is worthy of some discussion in and of itself. We draw some conclusions relative to three central themes in team teaching and learning for adult education: the relationship aspect of teaming, attention to task completion, and the underlying significance of collaborative knowledge creation. It is through our efforts and those of the chapter authors, as well as other significant work being done in various educational settings, that we hope opportunities for team teaching and learning continue to develop in the field of adult education.

Mary-Jane Eisen
Elizabeth J. Tisdell
Editors

MARY-JANE EISEN is director, workforce development, for the Connecticut Technology Council and the adjunct faculty at the University of Hartford, Saint Joseph College, and American International College.

ELIZABETH J. TISDELL is associate professor in the Department of Adult and Continuing Education at National-Louis University in Chicago.

1

This chapter provides a foundation for understanding the
nature, scope, and promise of team teaching and learning.

The Many Faces of Team Teaching and Learning: An Overview

Mary-Jane Eisen

When I agreed to edit this volume on team teaching for *New Directions in Adult and Continuing Education* (NDACE), I was excited about sharing my knowledge through writing. I knew I had a good understanding of the topic based on my research and practice. Because I had recently contributed a chapter to another issue of NDACE, I also felt that I knew the ropes. Yet my delight was tempered by a concern that nagged at me: How would I handle the workload alone? The obvious solution was mirrored in the very subject of the sourcebook. What I needed was a team—not just a team of contributing authors, but one particular teammate: a coeditor.

This got me thinking about my criteria for a partner. Recalling my experiences with team teaching in the classroom and my research on faculty development partnerships between peer colleagues, I knew that mutual trust and feeling comfortable together were essential. I wanted someone who had expertise and contacts in scholarly writing and editing, but it had to be someone who would view me as a peer, not a protege. None of my most trusted teaching colleagues was especially interested or experienced in scholarly writing, and although my mentor would make a wonderful coeditor, we would not be peer colleagues. On one hand, it would be ideal to partner with someone whom I already knew and respected, but I had also learned that productive partnerships can blossom between strangers.

In November 1998, I met with Elizabeth (Libby) Tisdell over breakfast in Phoenix, Arizona. During this informal meeting, Libby and I identified a shared commitment to the project, a feeling of personal comfort with one another, and a sense of complementarity, all of which have fueled our long-distance working relationship for the past year and a half. I had come to our

NEW DIRECTIONS FOR ADULT AND CONTINUING EDUCATION, no. 87, Fall 2000   © Jossey-Bass

initial meeting with positive feelings based on my familiarity with Libby's writing and philosophy. Meeting her in person transformed my hopes into a firm conviction that we would make an effective team. The only other time Libby and I met face to face was a year later in San Antonio, but thanks to extensive electronic mailing and occasional telephone updates, we have built a wonderfully rewarding partnership.

There is more to our story, of course, and in the final chapter, Libby and I reflect together on how our writing-editing partnership developed. For now, however, my goal is to set the stage for several snapshots of teaming in a variety of adult education contexts. These so-called snapshots portray actual examples of teams' facilitating learning across disciplines, cultures, and pedagogical styles. The chapter authors supplied them as a way to enliven the teaming process.

What Is Team Teaching?

Although team teaching occurs in many different contexts, models of it are most frequently drawn from higher education settings. Thus, as we seek to understand the teaming process, it is important to take a critical stance when looking at definitions provided in the literature, since they may not be reflective of the many variations that different contexts foster.

Defining Team Teaching. Davis (1995) offers this basic definition of team teaching: "All arrangements that include two or more faculty in some level of collaboration in the planning and delivery of a course" (p. 8). Davis adds that teams function along a continuum, and McDaniel and Colarulli (1997) suggest four dimensions of collaboration that might be used to locate teams on such a continuum: degree of curricular integration, degree of faculty-student interaction, degree of student engagement, and degree of faculty autonomy. This perspective of teaming as a collaborative yet variable process is valid, and it certainly represents many team-teaching arrangements well, but it is incomplete. Its subtle focus on teacher control and failure to empower learners blurs the essential relationship between teaching and learning.

I noted that this volume's topic was originally designated as team teaching, not team teaching *and learning*. This changed early on as soon as Libby and I discovered our shared conviction that teaching and learning are inextricably connected and that a key strength of the teaming process is that it generally serves to solidify this connection. Thus, we made it a priority to show not only how teaming can improve the delivery of teacher-centered education, but how it can extend collaboration to create practices and environments that are fully inclusive of learners. There are even some circumstances, such as popular or community education, where the roles of teachers and students merge, with teachers serving as facilitators or companions on the learning journey and learners assuming leadership for the direction and activities of the educational endeavor.

Goodsell and others (1992) put it this way: "Collaborative learning reforms classroom learning by changing students from passive recipients of information given by an expert teacher to active agents in the construction of knowledge" (p. 4). Team teaching may not be the only route to such reform, but it is gaining in popularity because it helps to dissolve historical barriers to teacher-learner collaboration, thus opening up opportunities for a richer multidirectional exchange among everyone involved.

Another limitation of standard definitions is their implication that team teaching and learning occurs only in formal settings, such as for-credit or noncredit courses. On the contrary, it often occurs in communities or workplaces that are not bounded by four walls or institutional structures, such as course credits. In our case, for example, Libby and I never entered a classroom. Rather, we teamed with each other and the chapter authors electronically to create this volume.

Making the Teaching-Learning Connection. Granted, most teaching teams consist of professionals whose job it is to design, deliver, and assess learning. However, based my own teaming experiences, the practice of sharing power with co-teachers paves the way for sharing control with learners. Hence, I have reenvisioned teaching and learning as a two-way process in which students teach and teachers learn.

To help learners explore their capacity to teach others, I assign them teaching responsibilities in the college classes that I facilitate. For instance, I conduct regular classroom research to elicit students' ideas on different teaching methods so that I may learn from their views on pedagogy. According to Cross and Steadman (1996), classroom research is a process in which teachers and students are actively engaged "in the collaborative study of learning as it takes place day by day in the particular context of their own classrooms" (p. 2). I also require pupils to do team projects in which they team-teach what they have learned from their primary and secondary research on a topic of their choice. Melissa, a graduating senior, recently captured the value of her teaching role in my class this way:

> This was one of the few projects that I got to work on here at the university where I . . . had control of what I wanted to learn. . . . Such an important take-away message for this class [is] that . . . the professor wasn't feeding us information [that she] wanted us to just spit . . . back at her. . . . We were able to present our thought[s] in our own way. Many times educators are forgetting that we are here to learn as well as teach during our education. I feel that the best way . . . to learn is to challenge our minds and give us the opportunity . . . to work on topics we like and present them back to our peers [Lai, 2000].

Similarly, I am acutely aware of how much I have learned through teaming by being able to observe firsthand what my co-teachers do in the classroom or how Libby handles feedback to authors. Noting both what works well and what does not work well over time, I have adapted techniques modeled by my teammates. Even planning a curriculum with one or more colleagues has given me insights into how to organize material and assess learning more effectively. I cannot imagine how these observations, modeling opportunities, joint planning sessions, and peer coaching experiences could be replicated in a formal faculty development workshop.

The Growing Momentum of Team Teaching and Learning

Although the literature on team teaching comprises only a fraction of writings on instructional innovations and collaborative learning, this modality is steadily gaining attention, for several reasons.

First, the democratization of education following World War II spawned a population of learners with more diverse learning styles than ever before—learners who gravitate to alternative educational formats such as service-learning and cooperative education. Teaching teams can respond to this demand for variety by introducing diverse teaching styles and expertise and by expanding team membership to include learners.

Second, technological advances have popularized asynchronous and self-paced learning by making them more accessible than ever before imagined through online classes. Partnering with technology experts or fellow explorers is an excellent way to ease teachers' entry into the new frontier of cyber-education.

Globalization, another key trend, requires the refinement of multicultural and interdisciplinary lenses for viewing and understanding our increasingly complex world. Many educators also believe that this trend calls for a more critically reflective stance, for example, by asking who is being served by the globalization movement: big business or individual citizens. Interdisciplinary or multicultural teams can enrich learning and promote critical thinking through their members' varied perspectives, while simultaneously modeling teamwork among diverse partners.

Perhaps most obvious, teamwork became a mantra of the 1980s and 1990s as business and industry looked to teams to reduce hierarchy, improve quality, and stimulate creativity in product and service design as well as complex, cross-functional problem-solving (Gibson, Ivancevich, and Donnelly, 2000). According to Austin and Baldwin (1991), collaboration is on the rise throughout American society as "workers, managers, teachers, students, citizen groups, and others . . . consider seriously the benefits of working cooperatively to achieve important goals. . . . [Our historical focus on individualism] is giving way . . . to a new metaphor that emphasizes interdependence and complementarity" (p. 11). Thus, the demand for teamwork skills has grown to the point that traditional educators have to take notice. Within the academy, for instance, pressure is building to deconstruct the convention of faculty isolation that persists, despite the existence of cooperative research projects and peer review of scholarly publications. An unexpected upshot of this trend is that team-based approaches, pioneered by popular educators and activists decades ago, have now gained credibility.

The Many Faces of Team Teaching and Learning

The overarching mission of most teaching teams is to improve both teaching and learning by improving course design or educational practice. Yet no two teams are exactly alike because they operate along a continuum representing countless variations in goals, team membership, and members' relationships. Teams form for many reasons. Some come together strictly for convenience or to comply with institutional mandates; others share a passion or cause; still others fall somewhere in between. Regarding composition, most teams consist of credentialed professionals, but increasingly learners are joining teams. Team members' relationships or ways of working together differ as well. Some co-plan extensively but teach separately; sometimes members co-teach, while others collaborate only to design assessment tools. Of the many ways to categorize teams, I posit one based on team goals and one based on team relationships.

A Goal-Based Typology. Each of the eight team types discussed here has a different central purpose:

- Interdisciplinary or multicultural education
- Collaborative learning
- Community action and co-learning
- Action learning
- Specialized delivery
- Professional development
- Research
- Writing

This list is not exhaustive, nor are these purposes mutually exclusive.

Globalization has fueled the rise of interdisciplinary and multicultural studies by challenging the unidimensional, Eurocentric views that prevail in traditional academic silos. Kleiner (2000) notes that although trend-setting areas of interdisciplinary study, such as American and women's studies, began in the mid-twentieth century, the past ten years have been a time of increasing prestige and enrollments. Indeed, in our field of adult education, interdisciplinary and multicultural education teams are flourishing because they are very effective in fostering "integrative thinking" (McDaniel and Colarulli, 1997, p. 19) and an appreciation of diversity. Having diverse team members model the blending of their own different disciplinary or cultural perspectives is eye-opening for many learners and for teachers themselves. Two chapters in this volume specifically address this type—one in the context of an interdisciplinary general education curriculum for undergraduates and one in the context of a multicultural training series for volunteers.

Actively involving students in the construction of knowledge is the focus of collaborative learning teams. In their team-taught classes, Cowan, Ewell, and McConnell (1995) blended interdisciplinary teaming and collaborative learning. They report, "Our joint planning sessions became interdisciplinary conversations into which we subsequently invited our students" (p. 127). By evoking what they call "a pedagogical model of conversation" (p. 127) and modeling collaboration among themselves and with their learners, this team broke down not only the disciplinary barrier between humanities and religious studies, but also the hierarchical barrier between teachers and students. A snapshot of a similar version of collaborative learning in a college classroom appears in Chapter Three.

Importantly, collaborative learning models vary, with learner involvement ranging from casual or intermittent contributions to core team membership. On the lower-involvement end of the spectrum, learners may participate in periodic classroom research (Cross and Steadman, 1996) by completing context-specific classroom assessment tools regarding the impact of their learning experience and their suggestions for improvement. On the higher-involvement side, learners may meet with the team regularly outside class to provide more extensive input.

Also on the high-involvement end of the spectrum are action learning and community action teams, where the roles of learner and coach-facilitator in the learning process are equalized. Interestingly, although their contexts and objectives differ markedly, community action and action learning teams have a lot in common: they generally work in live settings on live problems; both the professionals and the learners are core team members, with the learners often taking responsibility for charting the direction and intent of their learning activities, while the professionals provide coaching or facilitation; and learning is active or reflective (or both), not passive. Significant differences are that community action teams seek to inspire social activism in community-based settings, and action learning teams are typically engaged in profit-making endeavors, seeking to maximize productivity, innovation, or quality assurance. Two of the chapters contain contrasting snapshots: one spotlighting co-learning in a community action effort and another involving a team of coaches and their respective action learning groups in a workplace setting.

Specialized teams include experts who provide some form of special assistance, resulting in a different form of collaboration. For example, technology experts may be added to a team to facilitate the development of online courses, and subject matter experts may be recruited to teach specialized material. The Internet has given access to education for geographically remote learners, disabled learners, and others. As more learners embrace distance education, teachers need support to create and deliver online courses. In addition, subject matter experts are needed to meet the growing demand for sophisticated training in highly specialized or technical fields, regardless of whether the delivery system is the traditional classroom, the cyber-course, or a community-based learning project. One of the chapters presents a view of pioneering team teachers in an online environment, and another depicts a team of local specialists who cooperate to ensure that volunteer trainers are ready to meet both regional needs and national standards.

Bruffee (1992) emphasizes that collaborative learning "harness[es] the powerful educative force of peer influence . . . [that is often] ignored and hence wasted by traditional forms of education" (pp. 25–27). Many instructors are attracted to teaming precisely because it creates a social context among peers that promotes professional development opportunities and diminishes the isolation of the teaching profession. Indeed, several chapters in this volume reference the incidental benefits of working closely with peer colleagues. Clearly, for Libby and me, our work as a writing team afforded us many opportunities for professional growth through peer observation and feedback and the joint and individual reflection inspired by our sharing.

Teams that form for the explicit goal of professional development may take the form of a dyadic peer learning partnership (Eisen, 1999), in which two colleagues coach each other toward designated development or renewal goals, or a "critical friends group" (Costa and Kallick, 1993), in which a small group of peers engages in periodic idea exchanges. In some cases, very specific professional development outcomes are cited. For example, Robinson and Schaible (1995) note that reading material in each other's discipline opened their minds "to a fresh look at the privileged perspective accorded our own discipline" (p. 59). They claim they became more adept at experimenting with new methods, structuring class meetings, developing assignments, and critiquing students' work. Saltiel (1999) distinguishes collaborative learning partnerships from teams, asserting that learning partners "are loyal to each other, while team members may have loyalty to the project" (p. 10). However, since the project for development-focused teams is professional development and renewal, dual loyalties can emerge. This duality is implicit in a few chapters in this volume, where teammates develop an interest in their mutual development as a by-product of their collaboration. Also, one chapter specifically addresses staff development for volunteer trainers.

The last two types, the research team and the writing team, are not addressed in depth in this volume. Nevertheless, they are important because they are the source of much of the scholarship that underpins numerous fields of study. In research teams, professionals partner with each other and sometimes with students to conduct research. Similarly, writing teams may consist of professionals only, or teachers and learners working together to compile, assess, and document information, with a view toward advancing theory or practice in a given field. Again, I can point to Libby's and my coediting partnership as one that was enriched by collaborative teaming.

A Typology Based on Team Member Relationships. Teams may also be categorized according to how their members relate to each other and work together. Watkins and Caffarella (1999) identify four working-style variations: parallel teaching, serial teaching, co-teaching, and co-facilitation. In contrast, I identify six relationship-based types, using the metaphor of the family systems model.

In most family systems, variables such as the number of members, their degree of interdependence or independence, and the life cycle stage of the family (or team) will affect member interactions. For instance, just as the *committed marriage* is the preferred arrangement when a family is expanding and children are growing, committed teammates must work very closely when new courses or programs are designed and launched and when new methods are being learned and adopted. In contrast, the *extended family* offers less intensive support, much like an inclusive learning community in which broad-based sharing among individuals and teams is encouraged, but not mandatory. *Cohabitation* works in situations where convenience is the prime objective, for instance, when it is helpful to share designated responsibilities without engaging in time-consuming exchanges. Cohabitation may also be a good way for prospective teammates to test their compatibility prior to committing to long-term projects involving course development or experimentation with new pedagogies.

Table 1.1 briefly describes these three types as well as three others. The most appropriate type depends on the goals and context of a given team.

Conclusion

A hallmark of progressive educational and work environments is the capacity to foster inclusivity in learning so that people can be learners and teachers simultaneously, regardless of whether they hold the official title of instructor or student or, in the case of university-community partnerships, university worker or community member. However, exemplars of inclusive learning communities are in short supply. That is where team teaching comes in.

At their best, teaching teams are model learning communities that generate synergy through collaboration. Because the fruits of their efforts are often very visible and since team members' excitement is often contagious, they provide inspiration for others to engage in collaboration. Of course, teamwork can also present challenges, such as time demands or potential conflict among teammates. Nevertheless, as many of the chapter authors suggest, the advantages usually outweigh the disadvantages, and there are many creative ways to address issues that arise. Importantly, the experience of resolving such challenges can make team teaching and learning that much more valuable.

Robinson and Schaible (1995) remind us that the success of collaborative pedagogy depends on how effectively team members practice it. In their words, "if we preach collaboration but practice in isolation . . . students get a

Table 1.1. Team Types Based on Member Relationships

Committed marriage	Team members select each other voluntarily and commit to working closely over time.
Extended family	Individual teachers or separate teams exchange ideas and materials periodically, observe each other's classes, or commiserate.
Cohabitants	Each team member does own thing with own class; classes come together for convenience (for example, to cover for an absent teacher, share guest speakers, or view videos jointly).
Blind date	Strangers are matched by a third party, such as an administrator. This could lead to a committed marriage—or a one-night stand.
Joint custody	Two instructors share one section. Teachers representing distinct disciplines may be in class together, using a serial presentation or debating format, or they may teach alternating classes. Multidisciplinary partners, who agree to share most or all class sessions, may develop a blended presentation format.
The village (or nontraditional family)	The team is composed of learners and teachers who seek to foster a broad-based learning community.

confused message. Through learning to 'walk the talk,' we can reap the double advantage of improving our teaching as well as students' learning" (p. 59). Similarly, learners can become role models for teachers and each other when they employ collaborative methods successfully to teach in the classroom or to effect change in their workplaces or neighborhoods. The chapters in this volume provide vivid examples of how teachers and learners are creating new knowledge together through more collaborative models for adult education.

References

Austin, A. E., and Baldwin, R. G. *Faculty Collaboration: Enhancing the Quality of Scholarship and Teaching.* Washington, D.C.: George Washington University, School of Education and Human Development, 1991.

Bruffee, K. A. "Collaborative Learning and the 'Conversation of Mankind.'" In A. S. Goodsell and others (eds.), *Collaborative Learning: A Sourcebook for Higher Education.* University Park, Pa.: National Center on Postsecondary Teaching, Learning, and Assessment, 1992.

Costa, A. L., and Kallick, B. "Through the Lens of a Critical Friend." *Educational Leadership,* 1993, *51*(2), 49–51.

Cowan, M. A., Ewell, B. C., and McConnell, P. "Creating Conversations: An Experiment in Interdisciplinary Team Teaching." *College Teaching,* 1995, *43*(4), 127–131.

Cross, K. P., and Steadman, M. H. *Classroom Research: Implementing the Scholarship of Teaching.* San Francisco: Jossey-Bass, 1996.

Davis, J. R. *Interdisciplinary Courses and Team Teaching: New Arrangements for Learning.* Phoenix: ACE/Oryx, 1995.

Eisen, M. J. "Peer Learning Partnerships: A Qualitative Case Study of Teaching Partners' Professional Development Efforts." Unpublished doctoral dissertation, Teachers College, Columbia University, 1999.

Gibson, J. L., Ivancevich, J. M., and Donnelly, J. H. *Organizations: Behavior, Structure, Processes.* (10th ed.) Chicago: Irwin/McGraw-Hill, 2000.

Goodsell, A. S., and others. *Collaborative Learning: A Sourcebook for Higher Education.* University Park, Pa.: National Center on Postsecondary Teaching, Learning, and Assessment, 1992.

Kleiner, C. "Why the Walls Are Quickly Tumbling Down." *U.S. News & World Report,* 2000 (entire issue, America's Best Colleges, Year 2000 Edition).

Lai, M. Unpublished essay, University of Hartford, Mar. 2000.

McDaniel, E. A., and Colarulli, G. C. "Collaborative Teaching in the Face of Productivity Concerns: The Dispersed Team Model." *Innovative Higher Education,* 1997, *22*(1), 19–36.

Robinson, B., and Schaible, R. M. "Collaborative Teaching: Reaping the Benefits." *College Teaching,* 1995, *43*(2), 57–59.

Saltiel, I. M. "Defining Collaborative Partnerships." In I. M. Saltiel, A. Sgroi, and R. G. Brockett (eds.), *The Power and Potential of Collaborative Learning Partnerships.* New Directions for Adult and Continuing Education, no. 79. San Francisco: Jossey-Bass, 1999.

Watkins, K., and Caffarella, R. "Team Teaching: Face-to-Face and Online." Presentation at Commission of Professors of Adult Education meeting, San Antonio, Tex., Oct. 17, 1999.

MARY-JANE EISEN is director, workforce development, for the Connecticut Technology Council and adjunct faculty at the University of Hartford, Saint Joseph College, and American International College.

2

Effective structure plus flexibility are essential in the administration of a program that asks faculty to work together across disciplinary boundaries.

Creating and Maintaining Team-Taught Interdisciplinary General Education

Marcia Bundy Seabury, Karen A. Barrett

Interdisciplinary curricula are gaining acceptance across the educational spectrum because they develop learners' ability to connect diverse areas of knowledge. Students gain critical thinking skills as they explore the complex issues and problems of their world through multiple perspectives. Typically students from kindergarten through college enter the kingdoms of individual teachers, learning to see the world from a series of compartmentalized perspectives. Through interdisciplinary initiatives, they are learning more connected modes of knowing (Fiscella and Kimmel, 1999; Klein and Doty, 1994; Davis, 1995; Newell, 1998). Faculty gain as well through increased opportunities for collaboration and professional development.

A combination of interdisciplinary studies and team teaching is particularly well suited to adult learners. Adults' comfort with experiential learning that is not bounded by the traditional academic disciplines provides a strong basis for integrative, interdisciplinary learning (Dinmore, 1997). Further, adults' experiences on teams of people with varying kinds of expertise and competing perspectives are good preparation for the collaborative learning modeled by teaching teams. Adults have also faced the complexities of social, personal, and professional issues. Thus, interdisciplinary team-taught courses allow them to study in ways they have experienced as essential outside the academy. Access to diverse faculty who can help them connect their life experiences with the perspectives of multiple disciplines and compare and contrast those perspectives also helps them gain a more comprehensive worldview.

We have observed that educators today seldom need to be sold on the benefits of interdisciplinary education; what they want to know is how to do it. We are past and current directors of a twelve-year-old interdisciplinary studies program at a comprehensive university. When we attend professional conferences, conversations with faculty and administrators from other institutions often follow a predictable pattern. Upon learning of our program, colleagues respond, "What a great idea!" followed by, "But that would never work here," or, "We've tried that but it didn't work. We just never seemed to have enough [faculty, administrative, financial] support." A tone of frustration dominates.

As the conversations progress, we fill in some details, which often leads to an intense set of follow-up questions and even some "Aha!" moments: "How does your program actually work?" "How do you gain institutional buy-in?" "How do you afford team teaching?" "How do you form teams?" "How do you develop teamwork?" "How do you deal with dissension to your plan?" "How do you deal with institutional politics?" "How do you keep your program fresh and focused?" True, each academic institution has a character of its own, but our university is not an anomaly. Because we are confident that our experiences with these issues can be adapted elsewhere, this chapter presents our typical answers to these questions.

How Does This Model Work?

The University of Hartford's All-University Curriculum is an assemblage of approximately twenty-five interdisciplinary courses, all team developed and most team-taught, bringing together students, faculty, and ideas from across the units of the university. The courses are divided into five breadth categories; each course is structured to provide active learning opportunities and concentrates on the development of two essential abilities deemed necessary for educated undergraduates (see Figure 2.1). All students in baccalaureate programs are required to complete at least four of these courses, one from each of the categories furthest from their major. Most courses are taught in a dispersed team model. Two or three faculty from different disciplines come together once a week with their separate sections of about twenty-five students each for a joint discussion, debate, presentation, or performance. They also meet in individual sections once or twice a week.

How Do You Gain Institutional Buy-In?

Colleagues from other institutions often attribute their failed attempts to institute a university-wide interdisciplinary team-taught general education program to the fact that the change was mandated by administration. At our institution, change was driven from the bottom up and supported from the top down, an effective combination. Faculty frustration with existing general education requirements and compartmentalized disciplines, plus some faculty's desire to interact creatively and learn from colleagues, became starting points for discussions that eventually resulted in curricular change.

Figure 2.1. University of Hartford All-University Curriculum

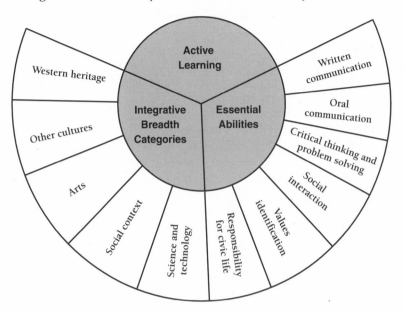

A sustainable program must also have adequate administrative support, including recognition within the institution, sufficient allocation of resources, and a cohesive structure for day-to-day operation of the program. Interdisciplinary team-taught general education courses need to be housed within an appropriate, and perhaps innovative, curricular and administrative structure that encourages collaboration across departments, divisions, and even colleges. We recommend a centralized structure with a designated director, the role we both have held, rather than having administrative responsibility dispersed across units whose primary loyalties are to their disciplines. This leader needs an independent budget and a strong voice in broader policy and budget matters, either through a position on the governing body (such as the council of chairs or deans) or direct reporting to someone with that position (for example, a dean of undergraduate studies). The program needs a particular office location with adequate support staff. Typical responsibilities of the administrator may include scheduling, faculty recruitment, oversight of evaluation, allocation of funds for instructional materials and faculty development, and relations with students, administrators, departments, and colleges.

In addition, responsibility for the program needs to be shared by faculty representatives from across the units of the institution, so that the program continues to be something "we" want, not something "they" require. A committee of representatives, chaired by the program director, can oversee liaison with their units and share in faculty recruitment and decisions regarding curriculum and policy.

How Do You Afford Team Teaching?

When an institution is exploring the wide variety of existing collaborative teaching models, it must consider the impact they have on resources. Team teaching is often defined as an expensive approach (Gaff and Ratcliff, 1997). A common solution is to limit teamwork to either the planning stages or early iterations of a course. The assumption is that as faculty work together, they become more conversant with the methods and materials from other disciplines involved in a course and gain facility in teaching it themselves. This approach, however, relies on a traditional model of solitary expert plus learners. If we want to bring our students into a more collaborative model of knowledge and problem solving, if we want them to experience knowledge as negotiated among different, perhaps competing, perspectives, designing team teaching as an ongoing part of the program makes excellent sense. But then we are back to the cost of two or more faculty teaching a single class.

Hartford's dispersed team model deals effectively with such pivotal issues as class size, faculty-student ratios, faculty time, and the calculation of teaching load while enhancing overall quality. Since team members have their own sections, they receive full compensation and teaching credit. This model effectively "balance[s] the values of faculty collaboration and all the benefits it brings to students with the realities of administering and budgeting academic programs" (McDaniel and Colarulli, 1997, p. 30). It acknowledges that team teaching does not equal one-half the work and should not be an overload. Students gain the benefits of meeting weekly with the entire cross-disciplinary faculty team and sharing in their conversation about the complex issues at hand while also having regular small group learning activities; faculty gain the opportunity to work closely with diverse colleagues while also maintaining a good amount of autonomy. Colleagues from other institutions who question us generally find that this model offers long-term sustainability.

How Do You Form Teams?

The best teams typically form in the faculty dining room, corridors, and offices, with plans formed from shared interest in a topic, such as urban ethnic arts. But an open call, for example, to a meeting to discuss a particular topic area, may also yield new teams. Or the director, committee members, or others may identify faculty who come from diverse disciplinary backgrounds but work on related topics, and link them to create a team. The literature contains many discussions of team teaching as similar to a marriage. Extending this comparison, one sees in practice that many arranged marriages can end up working as well as those born of long association and common passion. Some such teams will decide to continue work together over many subsequent years, having formed a productive collaboration.

("We've bonded," says one of our colleagues, rather surprised.) Other cases involve potentially provocative differences in ideas or teaching styles that look to make a wonderful mix for students—a biologist who emphasizes scientific objectivity with a sociologist who emphasizes the social construction of knowledge, for example, or a dynamic lecturer with an excellent facilitator of group projects—but after perhaps one attempt, faculty may not be interested in facing those differences day after day. At the very least, one has introduced faculty who could be on the same campus for years without ever becoming acquainted and sharing ideas.

As teams form, the director needs to be ready to deal with an array of practical complications beyond those typically involved in departmental planning. For example, the myriad pieces of university scheduling need to be worked out anew each semester, including the relationship of a team's schedule to the schedules of each participating department and the availability of rooms. All this can become a complicated task in institutions where scheduling can be equated with a house of cards or even gridlock.

How Do You Develop Teamwork?

For each facet of a course that the student masters, so must the teacher. Before faculty members can effectively team-teach an interdisciplinary course, they must become the learner, crossing the boundaries of their own professional discipline and expanding their scope of knowledge. As a team, they must work cooperatively with others to select and revise content, develop a syllabus, formulate objectives, select readings and assignments, and create evaluation tools. Faculty members have unique teaching styles, different comfort levels with the subject matter, and varying experiences in working on teams. They also have a varied ability to deal with group dynamics and to give and take to strike a balance that results in an effective learning environment for students. This scenario may appear to be daunting, but it is not insurmountable.

A wide variety of faculty development opportunities can encourage participation in collaborative work. One excellent approach, offering specific guidance with both content and pedagogy, is to have faculty sit in on a team-taught course the semester before teaching it (with a stipend or course load reduction if the institution can afford it). Another good option is summer workshops. Either internally or externally funded if possible (even a modest amount helps), these create a concentrated space for faculty to work together, read and discuss shared texts, plan, and evaluate. They enable the formation of new courses and new teams, as well as keep ongoing teams motivated and courses evolving.

Even with experience, many faculty lack confidence in their ability to help students compare and contrast disciplinary perspectives, design assignments outside their usual modes, and work well with other faculty in the classroom. We have held ongoing workshops, cosponsored with the campus's teaching and learning center, about these issues and many more. Arranging for workshops across collegiate lines amid competing meetings can be tricky, but even given fluctuating attendance, they keep important issues at the fore and attract good numbers of interested faculty.

Faculty need further support to make collaborative interdisciplinary work a regular part of their professional lives. Funding from the program for travel to professional conferences offers important tangible support. Our faculty now travel, sometimes in teams, to present at such conferences. Moreover, policies for promotion and tenure and for merit must support rather than deter faculty from engaging in collaborative interdisciplinary work. Faculty repeatedly cite the intrinsic rewards of doing such work but need to know that the extra time and effort they have invested will receive external recognition as well. Promotion and tenure guidelines and annual report forms can invite mention of collaborative interdisciplinary activities, and voices from outside the faculty member's immediate unit can be allowed key input during the promotion and tenure process.

How Do You Deal with Dissension to Your Plan? (Or, Does One Size Fit All?)

The best attempts at designing a program in harmony with the goals and politics of an individual institution and getting all constituents of a campus community to buy into it almost inevitably come up against the will of individual faculty members. Faculty development activities can win over many but not all. Amid the designing of our program, it became clear, for example, that one course team was composed of experienced humanities faculty who already felt comfortable crossing disciplinary boundaries and had no intentions of working together. Faculty on another team—and excellent ones at that—stated that they would not team-teach. One school of thought would be simply to muscle all these recalcitrant folk into line. But they would have simply withdrawn from the program, depriving students of the opportunity to work with some truly interdisciplinary scholar-teachers. The former team ended up meeting regularly, arguing out a couple of common texts each semester and sharing course materials, but teaching separately, while the latter has some teams alongside some self-contained sections.

Another kind of problem concerns the intended team of Person A who teaches Monday, Wednesday, and Friday mornings and Person B who teaches Tuesday and Thursday evenings. Neither can or will change schedules (sometimes it is difficult for an administrator to distinguish the operative verb here). The result in this case is perhaps joint planning and periodic visits across sections by each. Such flexibility can be particularly useful in a program serving both traditional-age and adult learners, since the time spread of courses is so great—often from 8 A.M. to 10 P.M.

Another variation is that after agreeing to try the dispersed team model, some of our faculty said their own teaching style made them never want to put more than twenty-five students in a room together. Some such teams may work out a compromise whereby they plan jointly but bring their sections together not every week but perhaps at the beginning or end of each unit, for special happenings staged by either faculty or students (for example, student presentations or role plays). Once again, forcing all faculty into a common mold can result in losing good faculty.

And then there is the other side: some pairs of faculty may have so much fun being in the classroom together that they do not want to split up for discussion groups. One of our course teams found that they enjoyed arguing with each other in class so much and that students became so drawn into the debate that they continued to meet with combined sections.

We have found that effective structure plus flexibility in practice makes good sense politically and pedagogically. We know many disagree and would insist on a single plan to avoid diffusion of program goals and ultimate entropy of the program itself. To the contrary, programs that insist on common practice can easily lose faculty support and ultimately be voted out of existence. Regardless of the eloquence of program goals and elegance of enactment plan, one size does not fit all and does not need to; a structure with stability may be the one that can bend a bit.

How Do You Deal with Institutional Politics?

To sustain a team-teaching program, the program administrator needs to be a proficient negotiator. In a curriculum cutting across the vertical structures of an institution, every course demands negotiation. Sometimes a long-term pattern results, with departments or individuals so committed to a course that they staff it semester after semester. Other negotiations are far less simple, for the fact remains that most team-taught general education programs rely on faculty hired, tenured, and promoted from within departments. It is of course possible to create a program with its own faculty lines, but many institutions will need or want to draw on the expertise of faculty within their diverse units. Indeed, bringing faculty together across boundaries, and thereby creating a sense of community, not designing yet another new department or division off in its own corner, was one of the goals of our program.

Faculty with disciplinary homes, however, have competing allegiances. Departments need to staff introductory courses as well as an adequate number and variety of upper-level offerings. Despite philosophical commitment to the goals of general and liberal education, the refrain from beleaguered department chairs and from some who are less beleaguered but also less committed to the program is, "I'd love to supply someone for the Adult Journey team, but we simply can't spare anyone this semester." And the refrain even from willing faculty members might be, "I'd love to join the team this semester, but we have no one to teach. Maybe next semester."

A supportive institutional culture in which chairs willingly allow and even encourage their faculty to participate is the ideal starting point. A director will still need to negotiate semester commitments. Various kinds of budgeting procedures can assist the process, such as funds to reimburse departments for adjunct replacement. Beyond this approach are a variety of both carrots and sticks to be considered within the political and financial situation of the individual institution—for example, incentive funds to departments whose faculty participate beyond a certain minimum level, or quotas that departments are simply required to meet. But an institution may lack resources for the former and may rightly see problems in the latter (such as a department's forcing unwilling faculty into interdisciplinary team teaching, with predictably less-than-optimal results, or a department's meeting a quota with its less strong teachers). The buy-in with practical follow-up promises better results than a strong-arm approach.

Some programs have been able to secure faculty through joint appointments with a department, or through having department-based faculty appointed as full- or part-time fellows to the interdisciplinary program for a specified length of time. The political climate of the institution needs to be considered with such realignment of faculty positions. Faculty may want to team-teach but do not want to endanger their status within the institution.

A part of the negotiations may be an acknowledgment that faculty availability to do team teaching will fluctuate according to student enrollment patterns and other external factors, such as accreditation requirements. Even as some faculty have to pull back to handle departmental courses, others may become available as the inevitable swings in majors leave their area temporarily underenrolled.

How Do You Keep Your Program Fresh and Focused?

The process of creating an interdisciplinary team-taught curriculum is never over. Inevitable faculty turnover, changes in research interests and teaching priorities, and so forth will cause teams to dissolve and even whole courses to lose their momentum, even as those same factors can bring new faculty into the program. Further, many teams go through a natural life cycle. At the beginning, everything is new and exciting. (To change the image and emphasis, one of our colleagues has claimed in print that the first offering of a team-taught interdisciplinary course should have a warning label on it. Faculty almost universally feel they need a second time to make changes.) But after a few times through, they may get restless and want to go off to new endeavors, whether a new team, new course, or new project entirely. Many particularly enjoy the early days of discovery, the serendipitous connections, before they feel they know what each other will say next. But other teams keep reinventing their course, changing materials and changing approaches. Many want to continue to work together semester after semester; when proposed a change, for variety, they respond, "No, we like each other; we're having fun."

Overall, the process of team building needs an ongoing proactive stance by director, cross-college committee, and the departments themselves. Otherwise the pulls back to traditional modes can hold sway. Indeed it is easier to teach a self-contained course within one's own department. And when faculty get busy with multiple competing demands on their time, the easier is all too tempting.

A variety of approaches in addition to the faculty development options can assist the process of ongoing team building. A university can specifically seek to attract faculty interested in collaborative and interdisciplinary work. Job ads for our institution typically note that applicants will have the opportunity to do such teaching. Departments can receive some leverage in obtaining faculty lines if either the new professor or current members of the department will teach in the program. Orientation for new faculty can include orientation to the institution's options for team teaching and interdisciplinary studies.

Finally, nontraditional programs especially need ongoing visibility and focus. As the original enthusiasm wears off and new initiatives divert both faculty and student attention, strategies need to be in place to keep both faculty and students aware of program rationale: why, after all, are they being asked to enter a classroom with two or three faculty representing two or three disciplines? Syllabi can contain explicit comment on how the goals and methods of a particular course relate to the goals of the program. Classes can take a step back from a particular discussion to consider issues of team teaching and interdisciplinary learning: "What are the implications of faculty's arguing with each other in class? Does it mean we don't get along? What other possible implications are there? For example, how do competing views of world hunger get negotiated into programs and policies?" University catalogues can give appropriate visibility to team teaching and interdisciplinary learning. A newsletter can reach the entire campus community, and a regular or occasional column can appear in the campus newspaper.

Conclusion

Underlying all our suggestions about the practicalities of creating and sustaining a program is a firm belief that the complications are worth it: that the solitary expert and an approach to important social issues through a single discipline are not the only modes to which we should expose undergraduates. A flexible team-teaching model should continue to be one of the options for creative faculty who want to encourage both traditional-age and adult learners to make connections across disciplines, their schooling, and their lives.

References

Davis, J. R. *Interdisciplinary Courses and Team Teaching: New Arrangements for Learning.* Phoenix: ACE/Oryx, 1995.

Dinmore, I. "Interdisciplinarity and Integrative Learning: An Imperative for Adult Education." *Education,* 1997, 117(3), 452–467.

Fiscella, J. B., and Kimmel, S. E. *Interdisciplinary Education: A Guide to Resources.* New York: College Entrance Examination Board, 1999.

Gaff, J. G., and Ratcliff, J. L. (eds.). *Handbook of the Undergraduate Curriculum*. San Francisco: Jossey-Bass, 1997.

Klein, J. T., and Doty, W. G. (eds.). *Interdisciplinary Studies Today*. New Directions for Teaching and Learning, no. 58. San Francisco: Jossey-Bass, 1994.

McDaniel, E. A., and Colarulli, G. C. "Collaborative Teaching in the Face of Productivity Concerns: The Dispersed Team Model." *Innovative Higher Education*, 1997, 22(1), 19–36.

Newell, W. H. (ed.). *Interdisciplinarity: Essays from the Literature*. New York: College Entrance Examination Board, 1998.

MARCIA BUNDY SEABURY is associate professor of English and former director of the All-University Curriculum at the University of Hartford.

KAREN A. BARRETT is director of the All-University Curriculum, associate dean of undergraduate studies, program director of medical technology, and director of allied health education, evaluation, and accreditation at the University of Hartford.

This chapter examines the challenges, benefits, and demands of co-teaching in higher education classrooms that emphasize collaborative knowledge construction.

Team Teaching in Adult Higher Education Classrooms: Toward Collaborative Knowledge Construction

Candace Harris, Anne N. C. Harvey

It was the ninth week of the quarter, and we were approaching the end of a two-quarter required sequence, "The Art of Learning." This course is designed to help entering students in Antioch's B.A. Completion Program examine how knowledge is constructed and develop competence in multi-cultural understanding. As co-teachers of this class for adult learners, we had decided to introduce Ricky Sherover-Marcuse's (1986) model of the cycle of oppression and alliance building, with Anne Harvey presenting the material and Candace Harris participating in the discussion. This class was to become an opportunity for all of us, teachers and students alike, in ways not necessarily anticipated.

As the presentation unfolded and we examined Sherover-Marcuse's assumptions and strategies related to unlearning racism, students began to critique the model. What then took place was unusual for our class in several ways. First, having one of us participate as a member of the group and the other in the role of presenter was a different approach to teaching this class. Second, although the plan for the class included discussion of Sherover-Marcuse's model, the depth and strength of the critique was a surprise. Many among this group of adult learners had expressed concerns about their ability to think critically in a college setting. And finally, although Candace was initially an active member of this critique, students directed the process of beginning to construct a new model with both faculty members listening and contributing to that discussion. Building on each others' ideas, they developed a theory that reflected their experiences with alliance building, oppression,

NEW DIRECTIONS FOR ADULT AND CONTINUING EDUCATION, no. 87, Fall 2000 © Jossey-Bass Publishers and unlearning racism. Together we explored the limitations of Sherover-Marcuse's ideas as well as new ways to work with issues of power, privilege, and the impact of racism on our own lives.

We reviewed a set of Sherover-Marcuse's specific assumptions about unlearning racism. The sixth assumption, which examines how people change their minds about deeply held convictions and asserts that if people are presented rational arguments they will change their beliefs, stimulated a particularly lively discussion about the conditions that are necessary for people to change their convictions about race. Here is how the discussion went:

CANDACE: I don't think logic is enough to change people's minds. Making sense appeals to a person's ability to think logically, but they also need to be touched, to somehow have an experience that connects them to what it feels like to be treated unfairly.

STUDENT 1: I agree. Presenting a reasonable position is not enough. My feelings help motivate me to change.

STUDENT 2: I have certainly had the experience of trying to help someone see things differently and have felt that no matter what I said, it was not going to make a difference. Something else had to happen.

STUDENT 3: I think people have to be willing to let go of their own power, to be able to share power, in order for these changes to take place.

STUDENT 4: We need a new definition of power, in which people have power 'with' rather than power 'over' each other.

STUDENT 5: Related to this topic of power, I do not like Sherover-Marcuse's choice of language. Her use of *allies, target groups,* and *on their side* reinforces a sense of adversity and duality rather than her intention to convey how we are all hurt by racism and need to work together.

As we reflected on this discussion, several questions emerged for us about how students experience constructing knowledge in a learning community:

As the perspectives of adult learners change, are they constructing new knowledge?

How does co-teaching facilitate adult learners' discovery of their own capacity to critique existing knowledge and offer new ideas?

How does a co-taught learning community help learners come to recognize that their frames of reference matter?

How can co-teaching contribute to students' learning new ways of thinking and to the creation of community out of difference?

These questions are at the heart of our ongoing reflective practice, our work as co-teachers in a two-quarter learning community. In this chapter, we examine the challenges and benefits of co-teaching in an adult education setting for students as well as faculty.

What Does It Mean to Construct Knowledge?

It seemed that we all enjoyed the opportunity to work together on a model for unlearning racism, articulating both points of agreement and disagreement. Students and faculty had paid close attention to the dynamics of race and power in this class, which can be simultaneously challenging, exhausting, and exhilarating learning, so this may have been a welcomed change of focus. We began our work together in the first quarter by examining the construction of knowledge, using the work of Freire (1995), Minnich (1990), and Belenky, Clinchy, Goldberger, and Tarule (1986) to help inform us. As teachers, we think about knowledge construction as the creation of a picture of truth informed by our experience, studies, formal and informal learning, and both internal and external sources (Belenky, Clinchy, Goldberger, and Tarule, 1986).

In *Beyond the Culture Wars,* Gerald Graff (1992) provides an excellent example of his own reconstruction of knowledge in his discussion of the impact of Chinua Achebe's writing on his own expanded understanding of Conrad's *Heart of Darkness.* Similarly, Minnich (1990) challenges educators to connect the quest for knowledge with life experience more effectively in her exploration of the false assumptions found in most academic material. She examines the effects of such "errors" as faulty generalizations and partial knowledge. Both Minnich and Graff examine the relationship of the knower to the known and recognize that all knowledge is constructed and embedded in a specific context worthy of examination. Belenky, Clinchy, Goldberger, and Tarule (1986) examine the process of discovery by women, suggesting that theories are not truth but models, with their own limitations. Thus, each of us as a learner is responsible for questioning, examining, and creating the systems that we will use to construct knowledge.

Another specific aspect of knowledge construction studied by adult learning theorists is what Mezirow (1991) refers to as perspective transformation. He describes the process that adult learners in our class experienced of reflecting on assumptions and beliefs, some of them deeply held convictions, which leads to changes in the ways they structure their systems of making meaning, which in turn changes how future experiences are filtered.

The Rationale for Co-Teaching

The Antioch Seattle B.A. Completion Program faculty designed this two-quarter course and decided to use a co-teaching model. The course has several intentions:

- To help students develop individualized degree programs
- To experience Antioch's philosophy of education in practice
- To help students develop a foundation of knowledge and skills in order to function effectively in a multicultural society

- To deepen students' knowledge and assessment of themselves as learners in the context of a liberal arts program

Collaborative knowledge construction is a central element of our work with adult learners. Together we explore the meaning of the liberal arts, what it means to become more educated, and students' assumptions about teaching, learning, and knowledge. The development of voice, empowerment through learning critical thinking skills, and the value of collaboration instead of competition in the classroom are central elements of this intensive class. We read poetry and fiction, and historical, educational, sociological, and psychological perspectives on the questions we are exploring.

Why do we use a co-teaching model? The size of the group (forty) is larger than most other classes (twenty) in our B.A. Completion Program. Not only is the workload then doubled for a single faculty member teaching this class, but the students have less access to this faculty member because they are one of forty to fifty students. In addition, students hoping for an opportunity to feel known and understood as learners by a single faculty member and seeking in-depth feedback would no doubt be disappointed. Thus, offering this class in a co-teaching format provides students with access to two faculty, which allows for the in-depth feedback they seek, as well as the opportunity to create a meaningful connection with one or both of their instructors.

Because these adult students are part of a nonresidential campus experience and have very full lives, it is not easy for them to feel part of a community. Therefore, it is our intention that this class provide them with the opportunity to be a part of a learning community, an initial cohort experience. We also want to help them consider what they have to offer and want to learn as part of this community. They receive feedback from their instructors on each weekly writing assignment, which provides them with thoughts from two different sources, further enriching the learning taking place in their first quarter. There is another reason for co-teaching this class. The benefits of co-teaching when addressing personally and academically challenging issues such as diversity, racism, power, and privilege are numerous.

Opportunities Inherent in Teaming

What then are the opportunities that co-teaching provides students and faculty that are not available in classes taught by one instructor? Perhaps primary among these benefits is the chance for learners to experience two instructors responding to the assigned reading materials and to the questions and comments that surface during a discussion—that is, to hear different positions. Although we share similar educational philosophies and worldviews, our individual responses value or privilege particular aspects of a discussion. We have been influenced by our distinct life experiences and different academic backgrounds, which affect our responses and positions. Because we each have our priorities, what we feel is most important for the class to attend to or engage with may differ. An example will clarify this point.

Later in the evening of the class we already referred to above, Anne came out to the class as a lesbian during the discussion of oppression. She consciously used this opportunity when students were engaged with thinking concretely about how to change assumptions about issues such as racism and classism in order to challenge their assumptions about her, someone they knew personally and respected. By using this opportunity, she modeled her willingness to be vulnerable and to demonstrate how one can be individually responsible during discussions of oppression. Her acknowledgment of this dimension of her identity challenged many of the students' assumptions about her sexual orientation and contributed to creating a sense of safety and support for other gay and lesbian members of the class.

Our assumption is that when students encountered this new information, they had to wrestle with their own homophobia. We knew that research has proven that people's oppressive attitudes are likely to change if they personally know a member of a disenfranchised group (Pharr, 1988). As co-instructors of this class, we had talked about the potential benefits and drawbacks of sharing this information. We had agreed that if the opportunity presented itself, Anne would make the decision whether or not to share this aspect of her personal life. She knew she had support, that she was not alone.

When students see instructors responding to concepts or theories differently, taking risks, and taking distinct positions in relationship to the material being studied, an implicit value is being lived out in front of them: that differences in perspective are beneficial to learning, acceptable, and encouraged. Diversity is experienced as being valuable. Learners having the experience of instructors' offering different points of view may become more appreciative of their own unique contributions. The banking method of education, critiqued by Friere (1970), whereby students are recipients of knowledge from an authority and expected to regurgitate the information on a test, does not expand their use of critical thinking skills, nor does it help them encounter their own power to construct knowledge, either on their own or with others. This important dimension of how we define learning is explicitly modeled in co-teaching, giving implicit encouragement to students to join the conversation and construct their unique positions as they listen openly to other points of view.

Teaming also provides the opportunity to model different ways of teaching and responding to conflict in the classroom. At times, one of us may challenge a student's perspective when the other may not have considered responding. In the class we team-taught, there was a significant emphasis on building a deeper understanding of multicultural perspectives. We found it particularly helpful to have two instructors available so that both could contribute during these difficult conversations (Graff, 1992; hooks,

1994), respond to students, and help facilitate these discussions. We found that students slowly began to develop a high regard for the diversity represented in the classroom and a growing sense of confidence about entering into these conversations. In our experience with the discussion of Marcuse's ideas, we witnessed the students' ability not only to challenge the material presented, but to offer what they thought and felt would be a more effective model of alliance building. They built off each other's contributions, respectfully challenging both the instructors and each other.

Qualities to Develop as Co-Teachers

There are inherent challenges in teaming in the classroom. As faculty, we have been deeply socialized to think of ourselves as the single authority. Although the idea of being midwives to our students was introduced in the last fifteen years (Belenky, Clinchy, Goldberger, and Tarule, 1986), many of us have not been challenged to share power with colleagues within the context of our individual classrooms. Co-teaching asks us to share both power and space with each other and with students. Although we may have invited speakers to our classrooms previously, rarely have we been asked to co-develop a syllabus, set class agendas, and co-facilitate each class session. Each of us is used to doing things our own way, shaping the class in what we individually believe is the best possible approach to the material. We may be highly dedicated teachers, but teaming is bound to challenge our equilibrium, disrupt our usual ways of going about our profession, and produce new ideas, perspectives, and knowledge about teaching.

The qualities and practices that we have found important in this enterprise are not surprising. In particular, we find it essential to allow sufficient time to develop a syllabus together that represents the learning goals that each faculty member most values. We also find it imperative to give sufficient time to planning class agendas and to debriefing after class. This investment of time creates a sense of co-ownership and provides the faculty members a time and place to voice concerns or make needed changes in direction or emphasis. The foundation for this dialogue rests on an ongoing discussion about each other's educational philosophy, a willingness to learn from each other's strengths, and a willingness to negotiate differences. We find it particularly beneficial to be able to voice concerns about teaming and to talk honestly about our hopes for and fears about the experience.

In a context where we are also trying to challenge the Western norm of individual learning, one of our intentions is to build collaborative skills and awareness of collective responsibility. We emphasize that each member of the learning community has a responsibility to contribute to constructing new knowledge. Seeing us demonstrate these skills gives the students a model of how to increase their own collaborative skills. Our joint construction of the syllabus and the way we share class facilitation and responsibility for feedback on student papers adds to this experience. When we express our appreciation of each other's contributions, respectfully disagree, or take a different position, we model ways to value diverse perspectives.

Challenges of Teaming

The challenges of co-teaching are connected to our values as educators. How do we negotiate the differences we bring to our planning sessions regarding what is important to teach? How do we focus our time and attention in class? We value diversity of opinion and of teaching styles, so we need to work with our own differences in the ways we work with our students' differences: by honoring the value of each perspective and drawing on the strengths of our ideas, thus constructing class plans that are better than either one of us would produce alone. There will also most likely be differences in the co-teachers' orientation to task and process. Some faculty are more task or content oriented, while others value attending to the process of teaching and the dynamics of the group. Addressing these differences throughout the co-teaching experience and ensuring that the two faculty members on the team have extremely opposing priorities in these areas decrease the potential for this to become a problem.

The time involved in co-teaching is significant. Because we value reflective practice, we agree to set aside time for both planning and reflection on each class. This reflection-in-action, examined by Donald Schön (1983), is a way of constructing new knowledge by critiquing an experience, constructing a new way of understanding it, experimenting with a new response in the future, and further refining this new approach. Our processes of reflection can therefore become ways of constructing knowledge as well. A foundation of trust and openness is essential to create an environment of learning and discovery for co-teachers. This can be a challenge to create and maintain, depending on the personalities and interpersonal skills of each member of the team. If the co-teachers do not share an interest in learning from each other, there will be a limit to the possibilities that can emerge in the teaming experience. hooks (1994) urges faculty to practice being vulnerable in the classroom, to take risks and learn from them, and to develop ways of teaching holistically. She sees this as a means by which we can grow and become more empowered, thereby facilitating the empowerment of our students. We believe that hooks's thinking about risk taking extends to our work with each other. We hypothesize that the more room there is for active risk taking and construction of knowledge in the work of the faculty team, the greater the likelihood is for a classroom environment that encourages risk taking and knowledge construction.

A final challenge comes out of our similarities. Given our similar worldviews, values, educational philosophies, and perspectives, how can we create opportunities that allow our differences to be visible in the classroom? We must consciously attend to this aspect of teaming in order to create opportunities to walk our talk about difference as a valuable aspect of learning and human experience. Exploring ways to use disagreements as educational opportunities is an ongoing aspect of our teamwork. Without a grasp of conflicting points of view and an understanding of a range of perspectives, it is difficult to become competent in constructing one's own point of view (Graff, 1992).

Conclusion

Our experience of teaming in the classroom provides us with rich material and invaluable experience to help us become even more effective teachers. We are privileged to see firsthand how a colleague presents her knowledge. We may learn new ways to approach a subject or handle a classroom dilemma. We have someone to talk with about our concerns if a particular class did not go as planned, if we are concerned about a specific student, or if we seem to be missing an essential ingredient in our class design or facilitation. If we are open to feedback, co-teaching can provide a unique and invaluable opportunity to see and to learn new approaches as educators. Although co-teaching demands a high level of commitment and effort, the rewards are many.

For those sincerely dedicated to the teaching profession, the experience of teaming can provide important insights into the practice of teaching, present challenges that help us make important changes, and provide our students with an even better opportunity to learn and grow. We look forward to continuing to work together.

References

Belenky, M. F., Clinchy, B. M., Goldberger, N. R., and Tarule, J. M. *Women's Ways of Knowing*. New York: Basic Books, 1986.

Freire, P. *Pedagogy of the Oppressed*. New York: Continuum, 1995.

Graff, G. *Beyond the Culture Wars, How Teaching the Conflicts Can Revitalize American Education*. New York: Norton, 1992.

hooks, b. *Teaching to Transgress: Education as the Practice of Freedom*. New York: Routledge, 1994.

Mezirow, J. *Transformative Dimensions of Adult Learning*. San Francisco: Jossey-Bass, 1991.

Minnich, E. K. *Transforming Knowledge*. Philadelphia: Temple University Press, 1990.

Pharr, S. *Homophobia: A Weapon of Sexism*. Berkeley, Calif.: Chardon Press, 1988.

Schön, D. A. *The Reflective Practitioner: How Professionals Think in Action*. New York: Basic Books, 1983.

Sherover-Marcuse, E. *Emancipation and Consciousness: Dogmatic and Dialectical Perspectives in the Early Marx*. New York: Blackwell, 1986.

CANDACE HARRIS and ANNE N. C. HARVEY are on the core faculty in the B.A. Completion Program at Antioch University-Seattle.

4

The online classroom offers unique opportunities and challenges for collaborative teaching. The example of two faculty members in an online master's program in adult education demonstrates both possibilities and pitfalls.

This Isn't Kansas Anymore, Toto: Team Teaching Online

Gabriele Strohschen, Tom Heaney

We are two members of a graduate faculty in a department of adult education, thrust with much forethought but little experience into the world of online teaching. Just as Dorothy, with Toto at her heels and her new-found teammates—Scarecrow, Tin Man, and the Cowardly Lion—prepared to face barriers and challenges along the Yellow Brick Road, so did we find strength and support in our team approach to the challenges of this odd new world. Traveling with a partner made the journey easier and more than doubled our resources in the strange digital environment we had entered.

Paving the Yellow Brick Road in Cyberspace

Team teaching reflects a growing awareness of world interdependence (Higgins, 1998). However, it is not always easy to agree on what constitutes the "team" in team teaching. There are multiple formats and approaches in teaching teams. Some have used a *star team* approach, in which one primary professor uses other faculty resource persons for specific topics. Others emphasize a *planning team* but then carry out their collaborative plan in serial segments guided by individual members of the group. At the far end of the spectrum is the *interactive team,* in which team members "share all responsibility for the class . . . and are present together in all classes" (Austin and Baldwin, 1991, p. 18). Our online collaboration exemplified the last approach to team teaching, in which we became co-discussants and co-learners with our students and in many ways modeled this new and different form of communicating.

NEW DIRECTIONS FOR ADULT AND CONTINUING EDUCATION, no. 87, Fall 2000 © Jossey-Bass

Essential to our success was a collaborative preplanning phase in which we developed some of the following strategies. Courses in our online adult education master's program are clustered in pairs. Students in the program enter as a cohort and take all their classes together. This format requires a high degree of collaboration on the part of the students and requires that faculty teams model democratic participation. As students enter our virtual classroom, they encounter a single syllabus that melds the content and objectives of two courses into a holistic learning plan. Our syllabus includes a weekly module, which contains a description of themes and issues to be covered, possible activities and discussion areas, and a list of online and other resources. The integrated nature of these cluster courses requires careful coordination and benefits well from the interdependence of team teaching.

Courses in many programs are put together like an assortment of building blocks, the connections and relationships between pieces serendipitously emerging over time. Choices are guided by an adviser, but also by convenience and availability. New possibilities emerge, however, when a learning environment combines a cohort model with team teaching. The cohort model makes it possible to plan the sequence of the curriculum carefully, and the continuity of experiences within a single learning group over time creates the opportunity to build on what went before and collectively reflect on shared, as well as individual, learning. Team teaching further invites the integration of curriculum, especially when two or more courses are combined in a single syllabus. This integration is especially important when learners are operating asynchronously and no longer have the visual and temporal markers of classrooms and class schedules.

We both welcomed having a partner in exploring the unknown terrain of a cyber-university. Our collaboration left us freer to abandon traditional ways of teaching, experiment, and risk failure. There was always someone at hand to help us pick up the pieces. In hindsight we recognize there were specific roles we assumed, mostly together, occasionally dividing responsibilities equally. The following vignette demonstrates how our partnership worked.

Conflict and Turmoil in Oz

Four semesters into the program, the student members of the online master's program cohort revolted. It was a somewhat gentle revolt of interdependent and collaborative dimensions. Nevertheless, it was a revolt that earnestly sought to redefine expectations and reclaim a power that learners felt they had lost in the online program. What happened to a relatively content group of online distance learners?

The course that semester focused on conventional and alternative organizational behavior and management belief systems, emphasizing leadership development as a means for empowerment in adult education organizations. In the fourth semester, careful attention and much effort had gone into the preparation of the syllabus with emphasis on the components described earlier. The paired courses, "Adult Education Leadership: Planning" and "Adult Education Leadership: Administration," centered on a case study. Both instructors and learners were able to select roles and tasks in a case, while retaining the option to propose an alternate course activity. We had offered the syllabus for review and negotiation prior to the beginning of the course. Feedback had been provided in the form of synchronous chatroom discussions, one-on-one e-mails, postings, and observation summaries. Now, near the end of the course, a week-long debriefing and analysis phase was to be ushered in, with the faculty team providing critique. We carefully designed evaluative feedback to the students, both individually and as a group, including an analysis that expressed our personal reflections on strengths and weaknesses within our interactions as a group of learners over time.

Our jointly written feedback had been composed after an afternoon of reflection and discussion as we mindfully considered learners' formative evaluation and feedback from the term. As a team, we had weighed our comments against possible consequences and misunderstandings. We knew we were taking a risk in sharing our analysis. The critique was intentionally designed to nudge the learners to review not only the content of the term's subject but also to reflect on the process of how assumptions—not facts—about power and authority had affected communications and trust within the cohort, including the faculty team.

When we posted this critique, the cyberspace classroom was filled with an audible silence—an absence of postings to the discussion board for a day or two. We learned later that learners had communicated responses to the critique in private e-mails and huddled prior to coming "on board" with their reactions. When the first postings arrived in the wake of the critique, it was clear that community building had taken place in nonposted interactions and that previous divisions among cohort members had been bridged in a sudden burst of student solidarity. They expressed support for one another and highlighted the contributions of peers, countering the "weaknesses" identified in the faculty critique. In the postings for the first time, students revealed and staunchly defended where they stood, and they aired pent-up frustrations. Initially they addressed their postings to their peers. One learner, however, who had been previously ostracized by several of her peers, understood and pointed out to her co-learners that we were analyzing our behavior and group processes in order to understand both course content (leadership in adult education) and unresolved power issues within the group.

Our critique, in part, analyzed our online communication process as a significant component of the course content. It had attempted to illuminate what each person had contributed in the asynchronous dialogue and how the cohort and its subgroups had been constructed over time. Over the previous terms, the cohort had replicated typical behaviors of members in organizations and needlessly maintained power structures, such as through acting on assumed distributions of stakeholders, "management's" authority, blaming, and victimizing.

The controversy over our feedback, though painful, provided a pivotal platform for clarifying online learning and teaching style preferences and assumptions about power and authority. Our critique broke the facade of the online classroom as an ideal and ethereal environment in which the usual struggles for dominance, power, and control do not occur. That critique, which emerged during faculty team discussion, integrated our reflections on content, format, and feelings. Learners had passed on the chance to negotiate the syllabus and assume leadership during the course when this option was offered several times at the beginning of the course. Although the online environment lent itself to switch easily from teacher-prompted discussions to student-generated dialogues, here in the mercurial virtual classroom a not-talked-about adherence to traditional teacher-student power structures was able to prevail unchallenged.

The critique and ensuing discussion provided an impetus to foreground the need for clarity, consistency of key format benchmarks, continuous feedback, and rigorous evaluation in a collaborative open team atmosphere. During the last two days of the course in term four and continuing for five days after the course officially ended, the posted discussion raged as learners took control. This term was the first one in which the previous discussions on power, participatory modes of learning, and collaborative learning were openly and thoroughly analyzed and plans made—collaboratively by students and faculty—for implementation in future terms of this cohort.

Unfortunately, a bittersweet taste of frustration remained for some students, steadfast in their understanding that teachers hold the ultimate authority even in situations where they seek to make decisions democratically. The unlearning of traditional student-behavior is difficult, particularly in the cyber-classroom. Nonetheless, the emergence of a democratic classroom in the presence of undeniable faculty power remains a goal. The expressed mutual support and modeling within our teacher team are aspects that highlight the critical pedagogy context.

Emerald City on the Horizon

Because learners online are encountering their peers and faculty at times most convenient to them, they have to do much more organizing of the curriculum than their counterparts in the face-to-face classroom do. The two or three hours in a scheduled face-to-face environment allow the teacher to focus the energies of the group, as the conductor of an orchestra does. Online the instrumentalists are dispersed in both space and time; their tunes are played asynchronously, needing to be sorted and rearranged later into a consistent and harmonious whole.

In the virtual classroom, shifting gears between two or more courses could be even more disorienting, if not chaotic. In such circumstances, the teaching team, by combining their materials into a single syllabus, can simplify the organizational task of online learners who are trying to find patterns and relationships in their asynchronous discourse. The faculty team communicated frequently by e-mail and face-to-face to develop an overall framework. Because the program design was modular, responsibility for drafting individual modules was divided, but with frequent consultation with the other team member. One of us had frequently taught one of the courses being clustered; the other had taught the other course. The resulting integration not only strengthened both courses, but has unquestionably changed the way each of us will teach those separate courses in the future.

Pacing the Journey. Folders provide a useful graphic metaphor online, organizing the materials and making visible the relationships between and among the various components of the curriculum. One important and well-used folder in our program is called "Student Lounge." It provides a free-flowing and informal discussion space in which students can carry on all the conversations usually conducted in the university's hallways and common areas.

Learners in the traditional classroom have their calendars marked with the regular pacing of weekly classroom sessions. Online time has no such markers. There is a tendency, unless milestones are created, for the time to adjust to each student's pace—some students moving ahead rapidly and others moving to greater depth but lingering behind their peers. The milestones we placed in the virtual classroom were weekly discussion folders. The folder for each week identified several themes for discussion. At the end of the week, the folder remained available for students to read its contents, but students could no longer place new messages within it. This simple device provided synchronicity and rhythm to the escalating dissonance of each learner's varied pace, and it kept pushing discussion into new areas of exploration. The arbitrary time limit imposed by the closing of the old folder paralleled calling time at the end of a face-to-face class. There was always room for continuing unfinished business in the new folder, but the old business was then juxtaposed with the urgency of new questions, new readings, new reflections from peers. Overall, this seemed to create the forward momentum needed to keep course work on schedule.

Both of us read all posted assignments and engaged in the weekly discussions. We kept the discussion moving and on topic by raising questions or pointing out gaps in the dialogue. This task demanded of each of us a weekly average of six to eight hours either online or drafting responses offline. At the end of each week, we both sent individual e-mail messages to each student with evaluative comments and suggestions for upcoming work.

Finding Continuity on a Winding Road. Paulo Freire (1970) approvingly cites Mao Tse Tung, who defines a teacher as one who takes what the student says in a disorganized way and gives it back in an organized way. The virtual classroom provides an excellent challenge for teachers to perform this function. Student and faculty discourse is scattered within and around themes in nonlinear and serendipitous arrangements. At the conclusion of each week, one of us would take all the messages placed in the week's folder and combine them in an organized narrative summary. There was tremendous power in exercising this function. The comments were recast through the lens of the summarizer's eye. This was openly acknowledged, and dissenting voices were solicited in the form of "Comments on the Summary." In addition, the concluding narrative could also identify (and fill) gaps in the discourse, pointing out not only where we had been but also where we were unable (or unwilling) to go. Questions for further discussion could also be identified. This organization of student comments by faculty provided closure to each discussion and created a sense of momentum throughout the term. The summaries combined teacher and student input holistically and provided concrete evidence of learning throughout the course. A full-text version of the discussion, which preserved each individual's voice, was also available. This document offset, and at times contradicted, the privileged voice of the instructor's summary.

Knowing Where We Are. A "Feedback and Evaluation" folder was set up in the Discussion area. Here students could voice their concerns and suggestions for change, or even talk about material they liked and found useful. Each week students had the opportunity to submit, anonymously, to a member of the group a "Critical Incident Report," a summary of what they liked, disliked, or felt most engaged or surprised by in the week's discussion. A summary of their comments was prepared by the student who received them and posted for all to see. Finally, at the end of the term an evaluation form was posted. This form could be printed out, completed, and mailed to an administrative assistant, who maintained the anonymity of student responses and prepared an end-of-term summative evaluation report.

These practices will change over time, and there is no reason to assume the methods we have used, generated out of our experiences and assumptions, will become the basis for anyone else's practice. There is an argument for achieving a consensus across any online curriculum, however. Changes in organization and procedure from semester to semester are likely to increase students' frustration as they struggle to relearn navigational and other online skills that should become routine over time.

For this reason, ongoing discussion toward a pedagogical consensus about these broader issues of organization and procedure is essential. This involves expanding the concept of team to encompass all of the faculty who will be working in the online classroom over the terms of a program. At issue are not merely negotiations over shared roles and responsibilities, but strategies for adapting our pedagogy to the demands of the technical environs of the virtual classroom. To the extent that pedagogical choices are frequently made based on what we as instructors are able and have the skills to do, familiarity with the strengths and weaknesses of learning online is critical to those pedagogical discussions.

Singing One Song with Many Voices

Dorothy and her friends found strength and determination as they sang "Off to See the Wizard" on the road to Oz. So also did we find strength and determination in the harmonies and rhythms of our day-to-day online teaching. In order to situate our team teaching in its spectrum of possibilities, it was important for us to ask ourselves about the type and level of our collaboration. Davis (1995) identifies some relevant questions for judging the degree of collaboration, which influenced our early thinking about online teaching:

Planning. Are all team members involved in planning? Is a democratic process for decision making used? Are some members of the team excluded in the final decisions?

Content integration. Have the multiple perspectives of team members been included? Are the resulting perspectives distinct—various points of view presented in sequence—or are they integrated into a new way of thinking?

Teaching. Do all team members participate equally? Do some have different roles? Do team members work in identifiable time segments, or is their work intermingled with that of their collaborators?

Evaluation. Are all equally involved in assessing learning outcomes and assigning grades? Where is the highest court of authority if a decision about grades is challenged?

Throughout the course, both the social order of the virtual classroom and our relationships with ourselves and with our students were negotiated and renegotiated in an ongoing effort to create a democratic classroom. Our collaboration exemplified attributes of teaching teams identified by Gray (1989):

Interdependence. We were able to set and achieve goals that neither of us would have achieved independently.

Encounter with new views and approaches. We learned much about both process and content from each other.

Joint ownership of decisions. We consensually made all decisions regarding the substance of the two courses and assessment of student work.

Emergent process. Our pedagogy evolved as we engaged each week in critical reflection on our practice.

Through face-to-face meetings and e-mail, we co-created a normative framework through which we coordinated our activities. Week by week, we arrived at a mutually agreeable approach, even while maintaining (and benefiting from) our differences in perspective.

Unveiling the Wizard

Team teaching in the online classroom provides a unique combination of opportunities and challenges. We learned as much from our negative experiences as we did from the positive. Certainly our belief in the importance of collaboration as a tool for adult learning has been reinforced. That such collaboration can occur in learning communities spanning great geographic distances is unquestionable, as is the fact that obstacles to such collaboration are no different from those encountered in the face-to-face classroom. How such collaboration is sustained and what it takes to overcome these obstacles in the cyber-classroom, on the other hand, may differ.

Team teaching can model the social construction of knowledge. Students are encouraged to value their own contributions to discourse as they observe the varied perspectives and respectful disagreements among faculty. Over time this can result in a lessening of professorial authority, consistent with the practice of adult education. Kulynych (1998) notes that a well-organized, smoothly operating classroom elevates student confidence in the teacher's expertise and that the presence of two teachers in the classroom disrupts this unspoken authority.

In the online program, each of us provided feedback to individuals on their writing. Differences in our evaluation of their work, initially disconcerting to students, more accurately reflected the social reality in which discourse occurs. Emphasis frequently shifted from seeking professorial approval (and an acceptable grade) to understanding the assumptions that underlie these differences. The thinking that divergent assessments tended to provoke was more critical, more likely to lead to a greater clarification of rationale for positions taken.

Letting go of authority meant letting go of part of our identity as teachers. To some extent, this was more easily accomplished in the wall-less environment of e-mail communication and postings on boards. There was no front desk for the teacher to stand behind. We became more explicitly learners—colleagues with our students in the construction of knowledge. In contrast, our authority, much more visible due to the written mode, as the ultimate arbiters and judges of student work at times contradicted our collaboration with learners in building the curriculum. Although it was less likely that we, as team teachers, would evaluate student work based on its conformity to our own positions, it is nonetheless true that faculty, and not students, opened and closed discussions and assigned grades based on faculty-determined standards. In the cyber-classroom such symbols of ownership of knowledge production and validation appear to carry more weight than in face-to-face settings. The challenge remains to find new asynchronously communicated ways of building a learning community online.

Seeking the Ruby Slipper

The contours of the virtual classroom make it dramatically different from the boxed spaces that give form to our more traditional pedagogy. The broad reaches of cyberspace, which encourage the integration of multiple knowledges, ways of knowing, and disciplines, also diffuse attention, shifting emphasis from "the point" of a particular lesson to pattern recognition within a pointillistic sea of information. Asynchronous communication and the absence of regularly scheduled face-to-face meetings beg for an alternative—virtual markers for the passage of time and visualized forms of interpersonal energy. Translating old lecture notes into Hypertext Markup Language will simply not suffice. The online teaching structures we jointly created allowed everyone to focus on learning.

As we sought to create a learning community online, we also had to recognize our own strengths and shortcomings as individual instructors and as the team. In finding the courage to take risks, disagreeing with one another in writing for all to see, and carefully assessing our own responses to postings, intellectually and affectively, we mirrored the challenges faced by the fellows who accompanied Dorothy. As a team, we were able to share our experiences with one another and model our insights for cohort members. In the end, we discovered that the wizardly technology of the cyberclassroom need not let us lose sight of our abilities to find "our way home" to an interdependent community of co-learners.

References

Austin, A. E., and Baldwin, R. G. *Faculty Collaboration: Enhancing the Quality of Scholarship and Teaching.* Washington, D.C.: George Washington University, School of Education and Human Development, 1991.

Brookfield, S. *Becoming a Critically Reflective Teacher.* San Francisco: Jossey-Bass, 1995.

Davis, J. R. *Interdisciplinary Courses and Team Teaching: New Arrangements for Learning.* Phoenix, Ariz: American Council on Education and Oryx Press, 1995.

Freire, P. *Pedagogy of the Oppressed.* New York: Seabury, 1970.

Gray, B. *Collaborating: Finding Common Ground for Multiparty Problems.* San Francisco: Jossey-Bass, 1989.

Higgins, T. "Evolutions in Higher Education." *Momentum,* 1998, 29(3), 12–15.

Kulynych, J. J. "Crossing Disciplines: Postmodernism and Democratic Education." *College Teaching,* 1998, 46(4), 144–149.

GABRIELE STROHSCHEN *and* TOM HEANEY *are members of the graduate faculty in the Department of Adult and Continuing Education, National-Louis University.*

5

This chapter focuses on the unique form of team coaching practiced by learning coach teams in the context of one public utility's action learning program.

Working as a Learning Coach Team in Action Learning

Judy O'Neil, Sharon L. Lamm

At the end of the first day of their action learning program, participants take part in a "last word" exercise to describe their feelings at that point. Reactions and anticipation are usually mixed—to say the least:

"I'm a skeptic from the earlier teams I've been on."
"I feel overwhelmed."
"What am I doing here?"
"I'm uncomfortable [anxious, apprehensive, confused, cautious, nervous, wary]."
"I'm looking for direction."
"I have mixed emotions."

At the end of the last day of the program, there is a final reflection and dialogue exercise in which participants share any last thoughts they have about the experience. The responses at that point sound quite different:

"What I've learned has changed my personal life."
"We initially were looking just at the problem. The learning coach would throw another issue at us, and we'd realize the learning needed to be different."
"I understand the importance of having a learning coach. We need someone in the organization to help us, and we need to help each other."
"I was surprised with the learning process. We learned ourselves. We got help when we needed it, but we learned on our own. We learned by doing."

"We had a good coach. So long as he kept confusing us, it would help."
"Today is one of the richest, fullest, most productive days I've had for a long
time."

In what kind of learning experience were these individuals involved?
How did a team of learning coaches help them to achieve this level of
change and transformation? And how did that learning coach team work
together to provide that help?

In this chapter, we discuss the unique situation of how a learning coach
team enables a group to learn rather than teaching them.

Action Learning

In the 1940s, the concept of action learning originated with the work of Reg
Revans in England (1980). It can be generally defined as follows:

> Action learning is an approach to working with, and developing people,
> which uses work on a real project or problem as the way to learn. Participants
> work in small groups or teams to take action to solve their project or prob-
> lem, and learn how to learn from that action. A learning coach works with
> the group in order to help them learn how to balance their work, with the
> learning from that work [O'Neil, 1999, p. 14.].

Action learning has been compared with project work, quality circles,
various forms of simulation used in management development, and other
kinds of experiential learning. Although there are similarities, action learning is none of these other forms of management development or work
(Revans, 1980).

Learning Coaches

A study has shown that learning coaches work mostly alone (O'Neil, unpublished findings) and thus have little experience in working in teams with
other learning coaches. And even those who had worked in programs in
which more than one coach was needed had little opportunity for interaction with one another, so were not able to form teams. As a result, little has
been written about the work of learning coach teams.

Whether working alone or with learning coach teams, a learning
coach's primary interaction is with the action learning group. Coaches use
a variety of skill sets in working with these groups to help them learn from
their work (O'Neil, 1997). Process consultant skills are considered an
important part of the learning coach's repertoire, but they are insufficient by
themselves (McGill and Beaty, 1995; O'Neil, 1997; Weinstein, 1995). Additional interventions that take the action learner to a deeper learning level

are required to achieve the level of change and transformation demonstrated in some of the representative participant comments that opened this chapter. Such interventions include encouraging and enabling reflection and critical reflection, challenging the groups' assumptions, and "saying nothing and being invisible" in order to let the group learn from their own experience (O'Neil, 1999, p. 181).

Learning coaches' skills and interventions also affect the workings of the learning coach team insofar as the team needs to take care of its own interactions by using process consultation skills and appropriate interventions. In addition, the varying beliefs about the learning coach role in action learning provide a view of diversity unique to this context.

The Context: The Public Service Electric & Gas Program

Public Service Electric & Gas (PSE&G), the nation's sixth largest combined electric and gas company, developed an action learning program in 1996 to help the distribution department learn how to be successful in the new competitive environment that was quickly replacing their former regulated, hierarchical world. The following objectives were established for the program:

Enhance the way people communicate and interact with one another.
Weave quality tools and behaviors into the fabric of the organization.
Develop and use problem-solving and coaching skills.
Develop an environment of openness and trust, and get conflict out on the table.

Over two years, there were nine separate sessions with over 250 participants. Each session averaged 28 participants formed into four action learning groups of 7 participants each. A learning coach worked with each group. The four learning coaches also formed a learning coach team. Each action learning group addressed an actual business project, sponsored by a senior leader in the organization. During the program, the action learning groups met for a minimum of six and a half days over a six-week period with their learning coach and additional days on their own.

At the end of the session, each action learning group proposed recommendations to the entire senior leadership team. Many of these groups were involved in the implementation of their recommendations after the end of the session. Some of the outcomes included savings in the hundreds of thousands of dollars through work restructuring, improved relationships with the community through outreach programs, and a transformed view of company-customer interactions, from providing customer satisfaction to that of building customer loyalty.

Forming Learning Coach Teams

Prior to each session in the program, three learning coaches were hired to work in that session. They were hired based on diversity of background and experience, and availability. The fourth learning coach, Judy O'Neil, played the combined role of program manager and learning coach throughout the program. These four coaches worked individually with an action learning group and as a learning coach team. During the course of the program, fourteen different learning coaches were used. Lamm was among these coaches. In the program manager–learning coach role, O'Neil provided an initial verbal and written orientation to the program.

Three meetings were held prior to the start of each program whenever possible. The first meeting was of the learning coaches themselves. In many cases, the members of the learning coach team did not know one another or had not worked together before. It was important for them to spend time together to understand one another's backgrounds and the strengths they brought to the program, as well as their perspectives and assumptions about the work of a learning coach. When it was not possible for these meetings to take place or when all coaches were not able to be present, the absence of the meeting would sometimes demonstrate itself as a lack of trust or misunderstanding of motives and intentions in the work of the learning coach team.

The second meeting was between the sponsors of the program projects and the learning coach team, and the third meeting was with each learning coach and the sponsor of the project for his or her action learning group. Although these meetings were less important in terms of building the learning coach team, they were important for the overall success of the program since the project sponsor can have a significant influence on the learning of the action learning group (O'Neil, 1999). The meetings were of importance to the learning coach team in that they mirrored the program design in which the learning coach team would work. The program design required them to work as a learning coach team in the learning community as a whole, as well as individually with their action learning groups.

During the course of the program, each learning coach team also spent informal time together. Most coaches had to travel in order to participate in the program, so there were opportunities for shared meals and discussions. Although the program was discussed, these informal gatherings also created the opportunity for personal discussion and stories that helped the learning coaches better understand how to work with one another.

Design of the Program

The design of the action learning program presented a unique challenge in working together as a learning coach team. In each of the six and a half days of the program, the four action learning groups came together as a large learning community, with more than twenty-eight participants, and then separated to work as individual action learning groups. This movement between the large community and the individual group was mirrored by the learning coach team's needing to work together as a team, then separating to work with the individual action learning group.

The large community came together for two main purposes. The first was for what action learning refers to as "P," or programmed learning. "P" is "the expert knowledge, knowledge in books, what we are told to do because that is how it has been done for decades" (Weinstein, 1995, p. 44). A number of concepts were provided to the community to help further the objectives of the program—for example, ways of dealing with conflict and a better understanding of self through looking at learning styles. The second purpose was to enable the individual action learning groups to share some of their learning with the larger community. This was done through exercises such as fishbowl discussions and community reflection and dialogue sessions. Each member of the learning coach team provided a part of the "P" learning and led one of the exercises for sharing learning, so it was important that there was a consistency within each session and across the entire program.

In each day of the session, the learning coach team also needed to work with their respective action learning groups as these groups worked on their project. During this time, each coach tried to create situations for learning in which his or her group could integrate what they had learned in the large community. In the design of the program, there were other concepts that were to be introduced on a just-in-time basis, that is, when the group demonstrated the need for the learning, so the coaches also looked for opportunities to introduce those ideas. For example, if a group were struggling in trying to communicate, a coach would offer the TALK model—a model that provides a way to integrate advocacy with inquiry in a business setting (Watkins and Marsick, 1993) as a possible way to resolve the dilemma.

In both the integration of the learning from the large community and in the just-in-time learning, the individual coaches often asked for their own coaching from the learning coach team. At lunch, at the end of each day, and in conversations between meeting times, the learning coach team discussed what they needed help or advice with and what was working well in their groups. A coach might discuss difficulty in getting the group to understand a just-in-time element and inquire how others had handled it. Another might relate a story of some particularly positive interaction between group members and what the coach thought the reason was, so that the other coaches might learn from that experience.

Because each learning coach was working independently with a group, consistency became problematic. Another kind of balance that needed to be addressed by the learning coach team, which would not exist if a learning coach was working alone, was the balance between the needs of the individual group and the needs of the program. Consistency and balance were addressed in two ways. One way was through the combined role of the program manager–learning coach. This role helped in a number of ways. First, it provided continuity for the program, from session to session and between the various learning coach teams. Second, it was a checkpoint for the learning coaches in each learning coach team for their questions, issues, and concerns about the organization, the program in general, and their interaction with their individual action learning groups. Finally, the role served as a pushback on individual learning coaches, as well as the learning coach team, by challenging their assumptions or decisions at strategic points in the process. It helped ensure that the work in the community and in the individual action learning groups stayed within the broad parameters of the program, while still balancing the individual needs of the coaches and action learning groups.

The second important element to the consistency and balance of work was the dedication of the learning coach teams to spending long hours in preparation, debriefing, and acting as sounding boards for each other. Once learning coaches began work with their individual groups, they became isolated. As a process, action learning can bring about much change and transformation, and in the case of this program, the change and transformation were significant for many participants. It is often within the isolation of the group that action learning produces these waves of change (Yorks, O'Neil, and Marsick, 1999). Despite the need for the isolation in the action learning group to provide the privacy and produce the trust needed for this kind of learning, the learning coach team benefited from being able to discuss what was going on in their groups with other learning coaches. These discussions enabled coaches to understand better what might be happening in their respective groups, especially in the context of other groups and the program as a whole. They also provided opportunities to garner helpful suggestions and support for dealing with difficult issues in each of their groups. As a result of this deeper understanding, the coaches were better able to sustain the necessary balance between work and learning.

Diversity in the Learning Coach Teams

The diversity of each learning coach team contributed positively in a number of ways. For example, varied age, gender, and backgrounds helped contribute to the strength of learning coach teams by providing a range of perspectives and experience. This variety also demonstrated the value of diversity to the participants. Ages within teams ranged from the early thirties into the sixties; there were both male and female voices in each team; and backgrounds included academic, consultant, and corporate.

Diversity in terms of learning styles, personality types, and personal metaphors provided the biggest challenge for the program and the learning coach teams. At times this diversity created interpersonal issues within learning coach teams. For example, in the Honey and Mumford (1995) learning style framework, someone with an "activist" learning style might have less patience for debriefings, while a "pragmatist" might focus on nailing down the details for the next large community "P" offering.

Similarly, within the Myers-Briggs personality type indicator context (Myers, 1998), friction occurred mostly between "judging" coaches, who seek closure, and "perceiving" coaches, who prefer to keep options open as long as possible. Because action learning by its very nature is a highly ambiguous process and each learning group is different, the action and learning within groups are unpredictable. Thus, judging coaches, who normally like to work in a planned, settled situation, sought stability at least in the learning coach team. They knew stability would not exist in their action learning groups, where, in fact, their task would be to promote ambiguity. In contrast, the perceiving coaches, who preferred to leave things open and fluid, were content to leave the work of the learning coach team open-ended and changing. The variety of styles and types among the coaches pushed and pulled at each other as new program elements were introduced, mirroring the real-life situations that the action learning group participants experienced in the program. The program manager–learning coach, as well as the other learning coach team members, would act as facilitators to help resolve the interpersonal issues within learning coach teams that resulted from these differences and individuals' struggles with situations not comfortable to them.

The last important aspect of diversity deals with metaphors that influenced the learning coaches' practice. In her research, O'Neil (1997, 1999) found that many learning coaches had implicit or explicit metaphors that helped shape how they worked with the team. Five distinct categories of metaphors were identified, based on the internal views underlying the coaches' practices. To capture these distinctions, O'Neil assigned a label to describe each metaphor. For example, the *Radical* learning coach interprets a significant part of the role as enabling participants to become empowered and use that empowerment to question and challenge authority. This view of action learning fits a more radical mind-set than that of development within an approved paradigm. The *Consecrated/Religious* coach has an underlying current of spirituality to his or her work and submerges or subordinates personal needs to that of the group. The *Deep Divers* describe their work as going below the process level of the group to a deeper learning level. They often see themselves as being highly intuitive in their work, so much of their thinking is below the surface. The *Legitimizers* conceive of one of their main roles as that of someone who is just there, thereby being instrumental in creating an environment in which people are free to learn.

In the learning coach team, these metaphors manifested themselves when coaches spoke about their work with their individual groups. The different metaphors, or views, of how they worked and why they did what they did with groups enriched the work of all the coaches. It could become problematic if the coach's metaphor was so strong that it adversely affected the program's objectives, however. For example, a strong Radical advocated against providing any of the agreed-on "P" or just-in-time learning, wanting instead for the group to be free to do what they wanted. There are action learning programs where this viewpoint would be appropriate. In the case of the design of this program, however, some "P" learning was necessary to meet program objectives. The program manager–learning coach had to make this point clear to the Radical.

What We Learned and What We Recommend

As we look at the strengths and weaknesses of the learning coach teams, we can see similarities between their processes and the processes of the action learning groups that they coached. Some of these same similarities were also found in another action learning program in which research showed similarities among the action learning groups, the learning coach teams, and the research team (Yorks and others, 1996). From these observations we derive the following recommendations on the components of this approach.

Forming Teams. The process used in forming groups and how well the groups move through the development of working together is important to learning in action learning. It was equally important for the learning coach team. The coaches needed to build trust, understand and appreciate one another's perspectives and strengths, and work together for the common good of the program. In this program, we tried to accomplish this through early team-building efforts—both formal and informal—and active self-facilitation.

Our experience suggests that it is important to treat the formation of a learning coach team with the same care and consideration given to the formation of any other team. Time has to be set aside and a process created to allow the team to come together and go through the stages of development. Trying to skip, or accelerate, this process can be costly in terms of good team functioning.

Balance. Action learning groups struggle constantly with the balance between accomplishing their task and learning from it. This balance is one of the key dynamics that the learning coaches help them to address. The learning coaches had their own balance with which they needed to contend: balancing the needs of the program with the needs of their individual groups. The learning coach teams, with the help of the program manager–learning coach, needed to ensure consistency across groups and across sessions of the program. Notably, however, although consistency is important, especially in a team-based program design, a hallmark of action learning is to be flexible enough to optimize whatever learning opportunities come up in the actual work of the action learning group.

The role of the program manager–learning coach turned out to be one of the key elements in the success of the learning coach teams. She was the interface between the organization, sponsors, and learning coach teams, ensuring the needed communication between these parts of the program. She also provided a touchstone for the learning coach teams. Without the consistency thereby provided, the work of the teams could have been chaotic and the success of the program endangered. This kind of leadership role is an important element, particularly with changing team membership.

Diversity. Diversity in the formation of action learning groups, which is crucial to learning, is equally important in the formation of learning coach teams. Diversity in the learning coaching teams provided access to differing viewpoints and ideas. However, it can also raise conflicts in team dynamics and program consistency unless the issues are purposively addressed. In this instance, both the learning coach team and the program manager–learning coach team played active roles in ensuring that the positive outweighed the negative.

Despite the additional effort that diversity requires in team building, learning coach teams and other teaching teams would be much less effective without it. Although different contexts may require different ways of attending to diversity, seeking it out will strengthen the program and team.

Conclusion

Any program of this size and complexity carries with it challenges inherent in its teaching and learning processes. Action learning programs have their own unique set of challenges since the learning coach teams are not actual teachers, but are there to help participants recognize the opportunities for learning. As in other teams, leadership plays an important role. In the case presented in this chapter, the program manager–learning coach played a critical role in forming and helping to facilitate the learning coach team by making decisions if the team was unable to achieve consensus and by serving as a liaison for the organization, program, and the learning coach team. In the end, however, a strong learning coach team was vital to the success of the program. One participant said, "I understand the importance of having a learning coach. We need someone in the organization to help us, and we need to help each other."

References

Honey, P., and Mumford, A. *Capitalizing on Your Learning Style*. King of Prussia, Pa.: HRDQ, 1995.

McGill, I., and Beaty, L. *Action Learning: A Practitioner's Guide*. (2nd ed.) London: Kogan Page, 1995.

Myers, I. B. *Introduction to Type*. (6th ed.) Palo Alto, Calif.: Consulting Psychologists Press, 1998.

O'Neil, J. "Set Advising: More Than Just Process Consultancy?" In M. Pedler (ed.), *Action Learning in Practice*. (3rd ed.) London: Gower, 1997.

O'Neil, J. "The Role of the Learning Advisor in Action Learning." Unpublished doctoral dissertation, Teachers College, Columbia University, 1999.

Revans, R. W. *Action Learning: New Techniques for Management*. London: Blond and Briggs, 1980.

Watkins, K. E., and Marsick, V. J. *Sculpting the Learning Organization*. San Francisco: Jossey-Bass, 1993.

Weinstein, K. *Action Learning: A Journey in Discovery and Development.* New York: HarperCollins, 1995.

Yorks, L., O'Neil, J., and Marsick, V. J. (eds.). *Action Learning: Successful Strategies for Individual, Team, and Organizational Development.* Advances in Developing Human Resources, no. 2. San Francisco: Berrett-Koehler, 1999.

Yorks, L., and others. "Boundary Management in Action Reflection Learning Research: Taking the Role of a Sophisticated Barbarian." *Human Resource Development Quarterly,* 1996, 7(4), 313–329.

JUDY O'NEIL is president of Partners for the Learning Organization, headquartered in Warwick, Rhode Island, and assistant professor and coordinator of the master's program in organizational management at Eastern Connecticut State University.

SHARON L. LAMM is president of Inside↔Out Learning, an adult and organizational learning firm, in West Chester, Pennsylvania.

6

The changing literacy landscape led a national volunteer-based literacy organization to tap the power of team-based teaching and learning for its volunteer development.

Volunteer Trainer Development in Adult Literacy: Using a Team-Based Strategy to Negotiate National and Local Interests

D. Todd Evans, Jane M. Hugo

We work as field service coordinators for a national literacy organization, Laubach Literacy Action, the U.S. program division of Laubach Literacy International. Like our four other field service colleagues, we provide technical assistance to a diverse, national network of member literacy organizations and individual members. Rather than looking at the dynamics of team teaching and learning in a classroom context, in this chapter we share Laubach's experience with team teaching and learning as a strategy to negotiate national and local staff development interests in the volunteer sector of adult literacy (Bingman and Bell, 1995).

The Learning-Teaching Context: Laubach Literacy Action

Laubach Literacy Action is part of the oldest and largest volunteer adult literacy organization in the world. Its mission is to help adults improve their lives and their communities by learning reading, writing, math, technology, and problem-solving skills. Laubach has:

- Over a thousand member groups in fifty states
- Thirty state member organizations
- Seventy-five thousand volunteer tutors who teach over 150,000 students annually

- At least one paid staff member in 76 percent of member groups
- Forty-one hundred volunteer trainers
- Approximately eight hundred people in the process of becoming Laubach certified trainers

Each local member group is autonomous in the way it meets the needs of its community. Each is also part of the historical development of adult basic literacy services in the United States in which community volunteers often outnumbered full- or part-time adult basic education professionals (Ilsley and Niemi, 1981), and the scope of adult literacy needs has changed with the increasingly complex definitions of literacy (see, for example, Chisman and others, 1990; Smith, 1998).

Laubach Literacy Action accomplishes its mission by providing support to its members and the adult literacy field at large. This support includes instructional and training materials, informational materials, technical assistance, grants, conferences, training opportunities, and leadership in literacy-related public policy arenas.

Laubach's History of Trainer Certification. Since the early 1970s, Laubach has had a process for volunteer tutors and paid staff to become certified tutor trainers and supervising trainers. To nurture the capacity of trainers and community literacy programs to develop a large cadre of volunteer tutors, Laubach Literacy established an infrastructure that provided a set of volunteer-friendly teaching materials, specifically *The Laubach Way to Reading,* a tutor training workshop based on *The Laubach Way to Reading,* and a trainer certification system to ensure volunteer tutors were trained according to standards set by the national office. Laubach required member groups to use its educational materials and conduct tutor workshops based on these materials using certified trainers. In these ways, trainer certification was controlled almost entirely by the national office and, by extension, local certified trainers who upheld Laubach's training prescriptions.

Team teaching and learning were important to the trainer development process as well as tutor training. Specifically, someone wishing to become a certified trainer would team up with a more experienced certified trainer as an apprentice. In addition, Laubach staff encouraged trainers to team-teach when they did tutor trainings.

Over the years, rigidity crept into the certification system from the national office down to many of the local trainers. Not surprisingly, many certified trainers perceived themselves or were perceived by others as wearing the mantle of Laubach's training authority. As a result, Laubach-certified trainers grew to operate independently of the programs they served, often creating a lopsided power relationship within local programs.

The Emergence of a New Team-Based Trainer Certification Model. In the mid-1980s and early 1990s, a constellation of issues coalesced in Laubach's work and became the catalyst for far-reaching changes in its certification system:

By 1988, Laubach had 667 member groups, up from 27 in 1969.

Adult literacy had a higher profile as a public issue, and public policymakers were taking an increasing interest in the state of adult basic education (Chisman and others, 1990).

Everything was more diverse: students' and volunteers' backgrounds, the sophistication of established programs, published instructional materials, teaching approaches and instructional emphases, and the array of organizations involved in basic education.

Legislative changes, technology, and the educational standards movement began to reshape literacy instruction (Tracy-Mumford, 2000).

The approaches to membership, tutor training, and trainer development that had served Laubach and its network in the past became barriers to innovation.

Seeing a need for greater flexibility and effectiveness, Laubach eliminated the membership requirement for groups using Laubach's instructional materials, enlarged the scope of its tutor training materials, and revamped its trainer certification system.

The focus of certification shifted from strict adherence to a fixed set of training prescriptions to the development of training skills and leadership in adapting national guidelines for best practice to local circumstances. Laubach supported this shift in emphasis by producing and disseminating new training and print materials (Laubach, 1992a, 1992b, 1993, 1995, 1996a). In addition to the *Laubach Way to Reading*-based tutor training materials, Laubach developed tutor training materials around noncurriculum specific teaching strategies (Laubach, 1994, 1996b). These materials gave literacy providers professional-quality training materials with the flexibility to design tutor training to meet their needs.

The revised trainer certification system, launched in January 1992, put team teaching and learning at its heart. As the certifying agency, the national office set broad parameters for the certification process and shifted much of the decision making to the local program stakeholders who form a certification team. Now each team organizes around the needs of the person seeking Laubach certification. It is made up of a Laubach-certified supervising trainer (or an apprentice supervising trainer), the apprentice trainer, and a representative from the local literacy program or sponsoring organization. The team meets to discuss the apprentice's learning needs and to design a plan for meeting them. It then meets after training events involving the apprentice to evaluate his or her progress. Once the team is satisfied that the apprentice has fulfilled Laubach's requirements and is ready to assume a training role in the program, it recommends the apprentice trainer for certification by the national office. Supervising trainers are responsible for teaching apprentices how to conduct a tutor workshop that meets Laubach guidelines, helping them to develop effective training skills and techniques, and evaluating apprentices. Program representatives are responsible for evaluating apprentices' skills to ensure that they will meet the needs of local programs. The representatives also advocate for support from the program and keep the program informed of the apprentice's progress. The program representative can be anyone who knows the needs of the local program: staff or board members, a tutor, or a student in a leadership position.

The certification team's principal goal is to ensure that volunteers involved in tutor training contribute to the overall effectiveness of the program's basic education services. The apprentice trainer is the learner, whose developed skills and knowledge gaps become the starting point for the team's planning. For example, the apprentice trainer may have experience as a literacy tutor but lack public speaking experience. The certification team (including the apprentice) thus devises a plan for addressing this development area. The plan might include other team members' sharing their presentation experiences, reading books related to public speaking, seeking opportunities for the apprentice to observe different presenters in a variety of settings, and identifying other resources in the community.

Laubach national staff believe that the local certification team strategy helps ensure that trainer development decisions meet its national standards of quality yet are responsive to the "practical organizational realities" (Cervero and Wilson, 1994, p. 118) of local programming. Local certification teams increase the participation of and input from the apprentice trainer, supervising trainer, and representative from the program; encourage learning by all three members of the team; and provide a better opportunity to balance organizational, staff, and volunteer needs at the local and national levels (Ilsley, 1990).

Benefits of a Team-Based Strategy for Trainer Development

According to a certification system evaluation done in 1995, 85 percent of the respondents thought trainer certification was a good indicator of quality training and they were better trainers because they went through the certification process (Evans, 1995). The new team configuration infused Laubach's trainer certification system and trainer network with renewed flexibility and responsiveness to the changing literacy context.

Provides Training Continuity. Once member literacy programs were no longer required to use the *Laubach Way to Reading*-based tutor training workshop, trainers were free to experiment with the design and content of the tutor workshop. For example, Dick called asking for help in his efforts to revive a literacy council in St. Augustine, Florida, that had been dormant for three years. He had fifteen to twenty volunteers, thirty students, and $30,000 of funding to start, and he was ready to become a certified trainer. He had three different published reading series to use but did not know how to train using any of them. Laubach staff gave him Maria's name (she was from West Palm Beach) as a supervising trainer and suggested that Dick call former trainers to serve on his certification team. He then recruited Carmella, a former trainer, as the program representative on his team. Requiring a certified trainer and a program representative on the certification team provides a structure in which adaptation and creativity can occur while still maintaining continuity in the program's training efforts.

Increases the Knowledge Base. Dick had no idea where to start. The two people he recruited to serve on his certification team provided the knowledge he lacked. Maria provided expertise in the latest training resources and techniques, and Carmella was a much-needed link to the program's past.

Speeds Up the Integration of Good Ideas into Tutor Training. Team discussions may stimulate an apprentice's interest in using role plays and point to the program's need to have tutors practice goal setting with learners rather than just complete a paper-and-pencil exercise. The team may support an apprentice in experimenting with an adaptation to the goal-setting portion of the workshop.

Builds on Strengths and Offsets Weaknesses Members Bring. In another example, Robert called asking why he had not received confirmation of his apprentice trainer status from Laubach Literacy. He had given his paperwork to his supervising trainer, but national staff could not find it on file. Further conversation revealed problems with the supervising trainer, Ken. He wouldn't complete the required paperwork in a timely manner; sometimes he didn't get to it at all, claiming that he was overworked. Robert did not have a program representative either. National staff explained the roles of certification team members and the likelihood that a program representative could take the load off Ken. In a follow-up call four months later, Robert indicated he had recruited Marti, a tutor, as the program representative. Marti agreed to handle all the meetings and paperwork. Ken observes Robert's trainings and helps with his technique. The trainer development process began to work better once the team worked around members' strengths.

Supports Self-Paced Learning. Apprentice trainers are free to learn at a pace that is comfortable to them. The certification team is there to provide oversight, assistance, encouragement, and the occasional nudge (as Marti provided to Robert and Ken) needed to make sure the apprentice stays on track.

Minimizes the Learning of Poor Training Techniques. Apprentice trainers are less likely to mimic the poor training techniques they may witness in other trainers when the apprentices have two peers with whom to discuss various training scenarios or the evaluations of their own training performances.

Integrates Training with Program Services. The certification team increases the likelihood that training reflects program services and does not develop along a separate track. Edna, a new program manager at Learn to READ in Kalamazoo, Michigan, sought help from Laubach when the certification process for Ruth, an apprentice trainer, got bogged down in a disagreement. Sue, the supervising trainer on the team, insisted that Ruth had to do a *Laubach Way to Reading* tutor workshop. Edna, the program representative, encouraged Ruth to incorporate information on a variety of instructional materials used by Learn to READ, as well as small group instruction into the training. In the five months following her first call, Edna used Laubach's "Guidelines for Effective Tutor Workshops" to guide discussions about the general training design with all trainers. Sue resigned over the issue, saying she was "not suited for training anymore." Ruth was assigned a new supervising trainer who understood Laubach's new standards. As the example illustrates, the dialogue between trainers and program representatives on the certification team often leads to tutor training improvements that meet the needs of the program better.

Models Team Training. The team approach to certification prepares apprentices to work with other trainers once they begin to conduct tutor workshops. Certification teams model such skills as negotiating (as in the Learn to READ example), division of labor (as in the example of Robert), shared leadership, giving and receiving feedback, constructive feedback, active listening and problem solving.

The Challenges of a Team-Based Strategy to Volunteer Trainer Development

Laubach encountered many challenges as it used the local certification team strategy to move from a centralized staff development model to a more participatory one.

Change Takes Time; Resistance Happens in the Meantime. It took a while for information about the revised certification process, including the local certification team component, to make its way to certified trainers in Laubach's network. The lines of communication within a literacy program are not always good, all volunteers do not attend conferences, turnover occurs, and people do not always read what is sent to them in the mail. For several years those likely to be certification team members—program staff, certified trainers, and volunteers—were at varying stages of understanding, acceptance, and implementation of the new system. This variation increased the demand on our staff as we responded to calls like those we have recounted. In addition, many previously certified trainers, like Sue in the Kalamazoo example, did not like (or did not understand) the more open guidelines and participatory team process of new system. As a result a number of trainers decided to leave the network.

Team Participants Needed to Learn New Roles. Under the previous system, supervising trainers mentored apprentices and enforced Laubach's certification requirements. Now supervising trainers were being asked to work with another person, a program representative, to make an informed, joint decision about the apprentice's readiness to be certified.

Program representatives, who may have had a hands-off approach to training, had to learn more about that aspect of their program. These team members needed new skills, knowledge, and attitudes to fulfill their new roles. Laubach developed workshops and print materials (Laubach, 1992a, 1992b, 1993) to facilitate this process, but in a field with significant volunteer and paid staff turnover, conflicts like the one between Edna and Sue still developed. National staff had to talk frustrated trainers, apprentices, and program staff through the ways that we envisioned the teams working. Programs had to develop a new balance of power between certified trainers, apprentices, and paid program staff.

Quality Control. Laubach made the decision to provide volunteer-based member groups with high-caliber training materials, guidelines based on best practices, access to support personnel, and a more flexible trainer certification system. Because local programs need to design training to meet their local needs, Laubach acknowledged that quality control rests in the hands of the local program. National field service staff now spend much more time with programs, such as the Literacy Council of St. Augustine and Learn to READ, that want assistance in adapting their training to meet local needs without compromising the quality of the training.

The evaluation survey done in 1995 left no doubt that trainers want control over the content and design of the tutor workshop to remain at the local level. Nevertheless, those surveyed worried that other local programs, left to police themselves, would cut corners with their training, resulting in poorly trained volunteers serving adult students (Evans, 1995). Member groups struggle with the responsibility for their own quality. Consequently, there is a continuing tension between the training framework constructed by the national office and the work of the local certification teams and tutor training teams.

Certifying Trainers in Emerging Programs. The team approach helps continuity and draws on the knowledge base that exists in the local program. The fact is that once control over the content of the tutor workshop became the responsibility of the local program and the certification team, it became dependent on these aspects. This makes it difficult for people in newly established programs to assemble a team and become certified. Without the help of former trainers Carmella and Maria from a nearby program, Dick in St. Augustine would have difficulty learning how to design and deliver an effective tutor workshop.

The certification system allows for the supervising trainer to be from a different program and serve on the team from a distance, but the participation of the supervising trainer is limited. Supervising trainers and apprentices who have participated in the distance process indicate they do not give or receive the kind of support they would like. Laubach is working to improve this process, but supporting new programs and trainers that are geographically isolated from more experienced ones remains a challenge.

Recommendations

National or regional organizations considering a local, team-based strategy to reform a trainer network might benefit from our recommendations based on Laubach's experience.

Make written support materials as clear and simple as possible. It is easy to provide too much direction when changing from a centralized system to one where a lot is determined at the local level. Describing every possible scenario can limit the benefits of a team approach—the creativity and dynamics of the team—and make the supporting materials confusing, leading to more national staff time spent explaining the process. The goal is to achieve a balance between providing enough information to limit questions from the field, but not so much information that it restricts team identity.

Be prepared to provide orientation and support. Using a team approach for staff development may be unfamiliar to many people. As our technical assistance examples showed, participants will be uncomfortable, will get stuck in the process, and will ask a lot of questions. This is okay. As participants develop their own understanding of how the team approach is supposed to work, they will start to find their own answers. Providing information on such topics as team building, personality styles, and communication strategies in any orientation will aid the process. An electronic database that catalogues the resources in the trainer network is invaluable in making appropriate resource referrals.

Be prepared to relinquish control. The dynamics and creativity generated by the combination of team members are among the benefits Laubach sought in adopting a local certification team approach. However, these same characteristics can become problematic when the team decides on a direction that the national body may not have chosen. The national organization can provide some guidance; however, it needs to be careful not to stifle the creativity of the teams.

Provide guidelines for quality. One of the ways to become comfortable with relinquishing control is to provide guidelines for providing quality training. It is important for the guidelines to focus on the desired results, not the process for arriving at the results. Laubach's "Guidelines for Effective Tutor Workshops" (Laubach, 1992a) inform the trainer about what Laubach believes a tutor needs to know and be able to do to be effective. Certification teams and training teams can determine what workshop design will work best for them using these quality indicators.

Stagger the implementation of a team approach. Once an organization decides to approach staff development using a local team approach, it should recognize that local staff may be uncomfortable as they work with their peers to determine their development needs, find resources, and evaluate and report their progress. Staggering the implementation of the team approach can ease anxiety about change and create a more realistic implementation time line.

Decide how to handle team problems. How an organization chooses to deal with problems or conflicts will have an impact on the success of the team approach. Patience with and understanding of resistance to change are vital here. One of the best ways to limit the number of problems is to outline the roles and responsibilities of team members. If conflict does arise, the appropriate people can deal with it on a case-by-case basis, establish a review board, and provide a procedure for teams to change their membership.

Conclusion

The local certification team strategy has improved volunteer training, strengthened the trainer network Laubach relies heavily on, and improved literacy instruction. This strategy opens a space for dialogue about national guidelines and local needs in concert with a focus on individual trainer strengths and development. The team approach gives local personnel a flexible and informed support system and makes Laubach a more effective partner with its membership. Whatever changes lie ahead in the field of adult literacy, team teaching and learning will remain one of Laubach's leading strategies in its efforts to help adults improve their lives and communities through effective literacy education.

References

Bingman, B., and Bell, B. *Teacher as Learner: A Sourcebook for Participatory Staff Development.* Knoxville: Center for Literacy Studies, University of Tennessee, 1995.

Cervero, R., and Wilson, A. *Planning Responsibly for Adult Education: A Guide to Negotiating Power and Interests.* San Francisco: Jossey-Bass, 1994.

Chisman, F., and others. *Leadership for Literacy: The Agenda for the 1990s.* San Francisco: Jossey-Bass, 1990.

Evans, D. T. "Trainer Certification System Evaluation: An Analysis of Laubach Literacy's Trainer Certification System." File document. Syracuse, N.Y.: Laubach Literacy Action, 1995.

Ilsley, P. *Enhancing the Volunteer Experience: New Insights on Strengthening Volunteer Participation, Learning, and Commitment.* San Francisco: Jossey-Bass, 1990.

Ilsley, P., and Niemi, J. *Recruiting and Training Volunteers.* New York: McGraw-Hill, 1981.

Laubach Literacy Action. *LLA Certification Manual.* Syracuse, N.Y.: New Readers Press, 1992a.

Laubach Literacy Action. *LLA Certification Team Handbook.* Syracuse, N.Y.: New Readers Press, 1992b.

Laubach Literacy Action. *LLA Supervising Trainer Workshop Leader Guide.* Syracuse, N.Y.: New Readers Press, 1993.

Laubach Literacy Action. *Training by Design–Basic Literacy.* Syracuse, N.Y.: New Readers Press, 1994.

Laubach Literacy Action. *LLA Trainer Workshop: Basic Training Skills Leader Guide.* Syracuse, N.Y.: Laubach Literacy Action, 1995.

Laubach Literacy Action. "National Quality Standards for Volunteer Literacy Programs." Syracuse, N.Y.: Laubach Literacy Action, 1996a.

Laubach Literacy Action. *Training by Design–ESL.* Syracuse, N.Y.: New Readers Press, 1996b.

Smith, M. C. (ed.). *Literacy for the Twenty-First Century: Research, Policy, Practices, and the National Adult Literacy Survey.* Westport, Conn.: Praeger, 1998.

Tracy-Mumford, F. "The Year 1998 in Review." In J. Comings, B. Garner, and C. Smith (eds.), *Annual Review of Adult Learning and Literacy.* (Vol. 1.) San Francisco: Jossey-Bass, 2000.

D. TODD EVANS is the training and state program coordinator for Laubach Literacy Action, Syracuse, New York.

JANE M. HUGO is the literacy instruction coordinator for Laubach Literacy Action, Syracuse, New York.

7

A culturally diverse team enhances the facilitation of knowledge, awareness, and skill development regarding diversity issues when working with staff, volunteers, and members of national service projects.

Team Teaching and Learning in Diversity Training for National Service Programs

Viviana Aguilar, Ginlin Woo

We are part of a national facilitation team with a human relations and diversity training and technical assistance provider. There are fifteen of us, of different cultural backgrounds (based on race, ethnicity, immigration status, gender, social class, sexual orientation, spirituality, and physical and mental ability), who work together as team facilitators to provide training on diversity issues. For several years, we have collaborated on numerous local, regional, national, and international projects that aim for social change, and community development and mobilization in many different contexts. In this chapter we discuss our adult education work around diversity issues with national service volunteers who work with grassroots communities around community development improvement.

The participants we work with range in age from eighteen to seventy-five, with the highest representation being white women in their twenties who recently graduated from college. Participants work as volunteers for one of the national service organizations for a modest stipend, for a period of at least one year, and are placed by the organization in grassroots communities. They are of different race, gender, class, sexual orientations, educational levels, and spiritual backgrounds. In our trainings, we deal with diversity issues of all types; sometimes class or educational status is more of a defining issue, and at other times it is sexual orientation, race, or religion. We try to deal with diversity issues that are the most pressing in the group itself or in the communities in which they work.

Most often our trainings are conducted through an initial day-long workshop. In preparing to work with a group, we form a culturally diverse

New Directions for Adult and Continuing Education, no. 87, Fall 2000 © Jossey-Bass

subteam from the fifteen of us to facilitate a particular workshop. The exact number of facilitators is proportional to the size of the group. There are always at least two facilitators, and often more, with a ratio of at least one facilitator per twelve participants. A culturally diverse team approach is crucial to the work we do, emphasizing cultural sharing, dialogue on cultural difference, cycles of oppression, personal lenses, common ground, and cultural competence. We also discuss concepts such as unearned privilege (the allocation of power to members of a cultural group based only on their membership with that group, whether it by race, class, gender, body size, or physical ability), ally roles and relationships, and systems of power and privilege. Effective cross-cultural collaboration has consistently been powerful, multifaceted, and dynamic.

Our Personal Journey in Context

Because the cultural story and life experiences of the team of facilitators (and participants) are central to the work we do, we begin by sharing aspects of our own journey around diversity as co-authors and as two of the fifteen possible facilitators.

We both share a history that influenced our need to pursue diversity work as educators. Our work with these issues is ongoing and is always enriched by our interactions with people who are different from us, including our culturally diverse teammates. How did we get here?

Viviana identifies as Chicana and grew up in a *barrio* of southern California, as the oldest of five children. Although her parents were born in Los Angeles to Mexican immigrants, they consciously made a decision that their children would speak Spanish before learning English in school. Viviana remembers feeling lost with non-Spanish-speaking teachers, but eventually learned English and succeeded academically. This early experience of feeling excluded in school because she spoke another language, coupled with other experiences of feeling devalued, stuck with Viviana and led her to pursue a career in teaching. Through her teaching in a bilingual education program, Viviana worked to create meaningful educational experiences for predominantly Limited English Proficient students. Later, her educational equity work related to language and culture broadened to include adults in many different contexts, in both North America and the island countries of Micronesia.

Gin is Asian American and grew up in Seattle's Chinatown community, the only female among five brothers. In 1968, she left college to join VISTA (Volunteers in Service to America) and worked for several years in a predominantly Puerto Rican–Latino community in New York City, where she was an educator, counselor, and community organizer. Over the years she has worked on many social justice issues, including housing and education litigation, and bilingual education as director of a community preschool and parent education program for immigrant children and families. Her ongoing community organizing and diversity work (including with service volunteers) are shaped by her prior experiences of working on educational equity: teaching Asian American Studies, serving on the Council on Interracial Books for Children, and facilitating diversity training in both K–12 and adult education settings. She has teamed with others on both national and international projects around issues of political sovereignty, substance abuse prevention, creating sustainable community initiatives, and cross-cultural collaboration.

In thinking about how our cultural stories have unfolded, it is unsurprising that collaborating and teaming cross-culturally have been our preferred mode for both work and play. Indeed, we believe that facilitating learning and sharing on diversity issues poses many challenges and opportunities that are better facilitated by a team.

Our Approach to Diversity Training

Our collaborative approach to facilitating diversity dialogue is influenced by practitioners from the community service and education fields and colleagues working for social justice from other disciplines and contexts. It is guided by the team's adopted Principles of Good Practice, which speak to our shared standards about facilitator behaviors and what we believe constitutes ethical practice for engaging with workshop participants. We are very intentional and disciplined about our guiding principle, "Do no harm," and exercise responsibility for facilitating dialogue about important issues. We always seek to create a climate of safety and respect, and provide a level of closure for participants prior to departing that fosters a sense of social justice for all. We promote a broad understanding of diversity and include dialogue about cultural experience based on gender, ethnicity, age, sexual orientation, socioeconomic status, immigration status, spirituality, and physical and emotional condition. Inherent in our approach is our commitment to grow as individuals and collectively in our ability to facilitate and live in ways that are increasingly respectful and culturally competent (Cross, 1988).

Some Core Concepts. Several members of our facilitation team have helped develop the core materials and activities that our training team uses. An important aspect of training is relationship and alliance building. In our work on defining diversity, we examine the concepts and manifestations of group inclusion and exclusion and unearned privilege, and then focus on how to unlearn prejudice, build ally roles and relationships, and increase cultural competence. It is more difficult to facilitate dialogue around some concepts than others, because understandings often are shaped by each individual's cultural experiences. For example, sometimes when participants reflect on unearned privileges (the allocation of power to members of a cultural group based only on their membership in that group, whether it be by race, class, gender, body size, physical ability), they are left with residual feelings of guilt. In these instances, participants are challenged in support-ive ways to become more self-aware and open to multiple perspectives. We then focus on the power of learning to be an ally (one who refuses misin-formation and mistreatment of others and intervenes on their behalf when one is not a member of that group). This helps participants focus on spe-cific ways they can act in new ways rather than being paralyzed by over-whelming feelings.

A Typical Training Event. Our diversity training most often takes the form of an initial one-day workshop. Typically, after an opening ceremony, activity, or ritual, facilitators introduce themselves, sharing relevant aspects of their own cultural background. They complete all the necessary overview and introductory activities that allow participants to feel grounded in what will take place during the workshop. Included among these early activities are review of goals and objectives, expectations, the proposed agenda, the development of working guidelines, and important opportunities to build relationships with all assembled.

Once the climate is set, participants engage in activities designed to help them explore several core diversity awareness concepts. They work together to achieve a shared understanding about diversity. After defining diversity, topics might include examining group formation dynamics, inviting participants to reflect on their own early recollections of differ-ence, and discussing ally relationships and concrete ways to be allies to others. Also discussed are ways to develop cultural competence and strate-gies for working effectively across diverse communities. We then may challenge the learning community to focus on acknowledging privileges. How many topics are covered depends in large part on existing group dynamics, time constraints, climate of safety, and so on. Eventually all workshops end with reflection and, if time permits, full-scale action plan-ning and opportunities to offer appreciation.

A Practice Rooted in Our Philosophy. The design of our structured learning experiences is heavily influenced by the philosophy of our program. It is also influenced by the culture and expectations of national service train-ing, along with the background, exposure, and group dynamics of the par-ticipants with whom we are invited to work. Our philosophy includes a commitment to meet participant learners as much as possible where they are with respect to the issues discussed, and not where we think they should be. We provide them with appropriate tools, information, structured experi-ences, resources, and facilitation processes that allow them to leave with greater awareness and openness, and inspired to pursue their individual and team's awareness building and confrontation of systems of privilege more capably. In short, a key objective is the development of their interest and capacity to grow as allies to each other and the communities they serve.

At this juncture, it's important to note that the terms *diversity train-ing* and *multicultural education* mean many different things to different people (DeRosa, 1995; Sleeter, 1996; Tisdell, 1995). These umbrella terms are generally used to encompass content that focuses on specific areas of difference, for example, race, ethnicity, gender, sexual orientation, or class. Approaches to facilitating diversity awareness and dialogue, however, vary widely. Some approaches do not address power issues, or the fact that some groups within the society have more structural power than others. These approaches tend to treat multicultural education and diversity training as mere vehicles for examining "differences" among diverse cultural groups (DeRosa, 1995), without dealing with structural power disparities, such as gender or race, that are embedded in societal structures. DeRosa (1995) notes that "a striking feature of the diversity avalanche is how rarely words like 'racism' and 'oppression' are used" (p. 4). Like Nieto (1996), Sleeter and McLaren (1995), and other multicultural educators, we are concerned with power differentials and view such "I'm okay, you're okay" approaches as inadequate. The historical roots of multicultural education are grounded in the 1960s civil rights struggles for social justice. As Sleeter (1996) notes, a number of more recent approaches have strayed from their original intent of multicultural education as "a form of resistance to oppression" (p. 9).

Our belief is that in order to address the hard issues of acknowledging power differentials and systems of privilege as sources of oppression, we need to work at building a safe, respectful space and a sense of community. This means meeting the participants where they are in their understanding and awareness of diversity issues, while at the same time challenging them to examine their preconceptions and biases more deeply. Our experience has been that diversity training that employs confrontational approaches, where participants are made to feel targeted, often do more harm than good. A core guiding principle of our approach is, "Do no harm." On the other hand, there is diversity training that focuses on "feel good" or "we can all get along" approaches, which "can lead to a lot of warm feelings but create little change. Our approach tries to help individuals let go of pain, discomfort and ignorance, without creating new pain for themselves, others in the group, or the organization" (Hickman and Woo, 1997, p. 4), while coming to terms with social inequities.

Teaming as Central

Using a team approach is central to our philosophy and all-around effectiveness for facilitating diversity dialogue. When members of our network convene as a team to prepare for training, we usually know each other and have already established ways to work and learn effectively together. Nevertheless, relationship-building activities are always part of our initial planning meeting, no matter how often members have been co-assigned. We begin with "check-ins" usually on four different levels: physical, intellectual, emotional, and spiritual. We work more effectively if we know what others have experienced since we last worked together. This background information allows the team to make assignments and take on roles sensitive to each other's needs and general condition. This team process reinforces our vigilance about building spaces of safety and support for each other and our participants.

Envisioning what will take place during the training creates many opportunities for members of the training team to consider diverse cultural perspectives in selecting topics, facilitation strategies, and examples that could broaden participant awareness. Further, participants often respond with increased interest and reduced anxiety when they learn that the training will be team facilitated. They also find the training more dynamic and relevant to their experience as more facilitators are added to the team.

Throughout the training experience, the team embraces every opportunity to model diversity and commitment to working together across cultural differences. Often the co-facilitation appears easy and very smooth; just as often, it is a learning experience full of challenges and important struggles. This active commitment to do our own work, while urging others to do the same, contributes an element of consistency and authenticity that resonates with our philosophy. The team-training approach is particularly important to facilitating dialogue on diversity issues because of the nature of the content and the intense emotions that are often stirred up for both participants and facilitators. The potential for conflict is always there, and having a team of facilitators to share in caring for the process, the content, and the participants at all times during a training increases the opportunities for participants to have their needs met.

In diversity facilitation no one ever knows what activity or discussion will trigger unexpected responses of anger, pain, or defensiveness in a participant. Sometimes seemingly low-risk activities spark painful memories, which are better handled with a team present. Past experiences in this arena have occurred during a simple introductory workshop activity like sharing background information on one's name. Participants have been reminded of painful memories of historic oppression, such as being adopted under painful circumstances or losing parents. During these times, the co-facilitators can step in and take the person aside while others ready to move on to other work may do so. And because each of us is in a different phase of our own personal journeys with respect to diversity issues, it is not uncommon to find our own "hot buttons" pushed on occasion. Sometimes it can happen in the middle of facilitating an activity when a participant unknowingly makes a comment that sets off a hot button. On occasions such as this, it helps to have co-facilitators to help one regroup quickly.

A team of facilitators who are grounded in the same philosophy but come from hugely different cultural backgrounds and experiences also contributes to story sharing and the use of relevant metaphors. With the skillful use of juxtaposed styles, tones, and rhythms that a team of facilitators provides, participants are treated to a richly endowed experience at the same time that they are encouraged to pursue their own. Quite often we use ritual and ceremony to illustrate points and facilitate awareness building during workshops. Our ability to weave such experiences together is critically dependent on the diversity within the facilitation team.

Many have commented that our working together as a diverse team also challenges assumptions and prejudices about the cultural groups we have membership in. After spending time with us, participants get in touch with the part of themselves that finds working on a diverse team desirable. They observe that our differences strengthen our effectiveness because team members' different styles are also complementary. They sense the power of the teaming strategy and what it could mean for their own work in programs with communities. This is a very exciting aspect of our work, for both us and participants.

Assessment of Teaming for Diversity Training

Teaching for diversity is difficult work. It is often emotionally laden and occasionally conceptually difficult. But it is also tremendously rewarding. In spite of the intensity, participants' feedback on our workshops is much more often positive than not. Our facilitation team also feels good about our work together. Our own perception of "good" is when people leave a training experience with greater understanding and commitment to work across differences. "Good" is when they are more willing to examine their own issues around diversity, both as individuals and with each other, when they are more reflective about both their own privileges and their own pain. "Good" is when they tell us they feel supported in their efforts at being better allies and better able to integrate diversity work into their team process throughout the year beyond the workshop. Many leave feeling encouraged and hopeful that they and their teammates will work together to understand better how their prejudices affect their work.

Participants often forward very positive posttraining comments. They appreciate and sometimes also express their awe over the team-training experience. Many comment on the open and respectful climate that enabled them to talk and listen in ways they previously thought not possible. We attribute this ability to create and maintain such a climate specifically to the team facilitation strategy. When we hear this, we feel encouraged that others will pursue opportunities to collaborate across cultural experiences with greater openness and passion. The team process has afforded us the opportunity to model a vision of collaborative work that is directly relevant to the experience of the participants.

The team experience benefits more than the participants. The feedback from team facilitators is often equally compelling, with team members celebrating their own ongoing learning, as well as the fact that there are more opportunities for dynamic coverage of workshop content. In culturally diverse facilitation teams, there is also greater opportunity to model diversity by employing contrasting facilitation styles that correspond to cultural practices and cultural ways of knowing and learning. For example, in many cultures, the oral tradition is integral to teaching and learning. When a team member is from an oral tradition, a whole different tone is set in our workshop around teaching a point through story. As a diverse team, we also increase our chances to reach more of the participants in meaningful or connected ways, while responding to different learning styles, cultural differences, and similarities. We also learn from the multiple perspectives of our team in understanding participants' needs and different ways to approach the content. The reality is that sometimes there will be participants whom we as individuals cannot seem to reach. During those times, it helps to use the resources of our co-facilitators to help us make connections.

The facilitation team network has become more committed to all the processes we have described for our collaborative diversity awareness facilitation work. The opportunities to team together have affected each of us, so that the depth, breadth, and scope of what we have confidence to explore with participants have been dramatically altered. Not everyone in the field who works to build cultural competence and diversity awareness uses team teaching; however, for our work, we see no other option.

Conclusion

In the light of our own experiences using a team approach to diversity training, what recommendations can we make to adult educators doing this work? First, and most obvious, we believe that a culturally diverse team is crucial. It increases the possibilities that all workshop participants will learn and share from more diverse points of view, styles, orientations, and cultural experiences.

Second, we believe that sharing knowledge at all levels within a learning community is part of the work of equity. When the purpose is to help participants examine power dynamics within the society, a culturally diverse team increases the likelihood that the power and knowledge traditionally held by the teacher are restructured and shared at all levels in a particular learning setting.

Third, we believe that effective facilitators must support each other in working on their own issues around diversity. The check-in time for facilitators who are working together is never time wasted. Such time also acknowledges that the work of diversity is a life journey and is an emotional, spiritual, and action-oriented endeavor, not just an intellectual activity. Team facilitation and check-in time allows facilitators to create and maintain the climate necessary to continue their own journey and for authentic communication in diversity dialogue to occur in the planning phase and in the workshop itself.

Fourth, it is important to take adequate time to develop a safe and open climate. This foundational climate will be challenged when conflict erupts or when what is shared (usually unknowingly) by someone is experienced as insensitive to specific groups. This can pose a threat to the atmosphere of the learning environment, but if adequate time is spent developing it at the beginning, groups usually can work through such conflicts. Furthermore, during our workshops where concerted effort is made to create a safe climate for diversity dialogue, individuals frequently share and disclose much more and at much deeper levels than originally intended.

Using team teaching and facilitation strengthens opportunities for workshop participants to discuss and experience cross-cultural collaboration and ally relationships. This is the central work of diversity in adult education. To paraphrase Gandhi, we must live the peace we dream of. Walking our talk is critical to building trust and facilitating diversity dialogue and, ultimately, making personal, community, and societal change. We more than suspect that cross-cultural teaming and ally relationships beget more cross-cultural teaming and ally relationships. And this is where education for social change truly happens.

References

Cross, T. "Services to Minority Populations: Cultural Competency Continuum." *Focal Point,* 1988, *3,* 1.

DeRosa, P. "Social Change or Status Quo? Implications of Diversity Training Models." *Fourth R,* 1995, *56,* 4–13.

Hickman, J., and Woo, G. *Proposal for Human Relations and Diversity Training and Technical Assistance Project: A Cooperative Agreement Between the Corporation for National Service and CHP International.* Oak Park, Ill.: CHP International, 1997.

Nieto, S. *Affirming Diversity: The Sociopolitical Context of Multicultural Education.* White Plains, N.Y.: Longman, 1996.

Sleeter, C. E. *Multicultural Education as Social Activism.* Albany: State University of New York Press, 1996.

Sleeter, C. E., and McLaren, P. L. (eds.). *Multicultural Education, Critical Pedagogy, and the Politics of Difference.* Albany: State University of New York Press, 1995.

Tisdell, E. J. *Creating Inclusive Adult Learning Environments: Insights from Multicultural Education and Feminist Pedagogy.* Columbus, Ohio: ERIC Clearinghouse on Adult, Career, and Vocational Education, 1995.

VIVIANA AGUILAR *and* GINLIN WOO *are consultants with national and international human relations and diversity training/technical assistance providers. They both live in Seattle, Washington.*

8

Co-learning is a form of learning with and in grassroots communities that challenges power relations between dominant and oppressed groups, as well as the notions of expert and novice, teacher, and learner.

Co-Learning in the Community

Regina M. Curry, Phyllis Cunningham

In 1996, five community-based organizations, part of the Calumet Communities Consortium on Chicago's South Side, invited Northern Illinois University to join them in a bottom-up leadership development project, grounded in the interest of the primarily African American and Latino Calumet Communities. We are among several university workers who were involved. We are activist-scholars: Regina has spent her life in social struggle in Chicago's Woodlawn community and now is a doctoral candidate in adult education; Phyllis has spent the past thirty years as a social activist starting with her doctoral studies during the late 1960s and now as a professor of adult education. Regina is African American; Phyllis is Irish American. Together we are involved in several projects, but it is our work in the Calumet Communities where we have been co-learning with the community for the last three years on which we base this chapter. Through our work here we have developed the concept of co-learning, a form of learning with and in communities, grounded in the direct attempt to challenge power relations between dominant and oppressed groups and the notions of expert and novice, teacher and learner.

Early on, issues developed among and between community and university workers within the project that caused us as a group of university workers and community members either to learn or leave the project. For example, one of the community-based organization (CBO) directors, Lyn, had struggled ten years to win National and State Heritage status for the North Pullman community. Her dream was to develop a cultural tourism and entrepreneurial activity around the story of A. Phillip Randolph and the Pullman porters. Randolph started the first African American labor union after being denied membership to the white union. The Pullman Porters were the communication lines between the South and North before and during the great migration. A black university worker and graduate student proposed doing interviews with the aging Pullman porters and to develop a video from the interviews. Lyn agreed but asked if we (the university) could do professional production quality. We agreed, and the graduate student university worker organized the production.

At the first shoot, all kinds of problems developed. Who was to be listed as producer? Who would own the copyright? Who would do the interviewing? Those in the community wanted more control. The student felt that she had done the work and gotten the university media production there and had arranged for an interviewer. In the end, both Lyn and the student organizer were listed as producers, and the video was made with the proposed interviewer who knew a lot about Pullman but had not been involved in the development of the film, and so the interviews were not the best. Although there was surface agreement, no one won in this project: the university technicians felt that their expertise had been wasted, the opportunity to make a quality film on the aging porters was lost, and the A. Phillip Randolph Museum lost a resource that could have contributed to the cultural historical record of its community.

Nevertheless, we learned a lot from this initial experience, and in the year that followed, members of our co-learning community successfully made a film about the A. Phillip Randolph Museum. Team members learned that how each organized her life within a particular cultural context had to be respected. While university workers were wedded to the instruments of watches, calendars, and "real time," community residents were oriented to the rhythm of daily life such as clinic visits and an understanding of the clock in which time could expand depending on what was happening. University workers wanted a clear plan of goal setting, implementing, and evaluating. Community workers built their activities around symbolic events that they themselves had created: the Bud Biliken Parade, Kwanza Fest in the Park, Teen's Spring Fashion Show, and the Pullman Porters' Blues Festival.

Power issues arose when project money became available. University workers often could not see the accomplishment of the community workers, and community workers often felt that university workers' ideas were irrelevant. In the end, those who persevered developed a deep respect for each other and about what we had learned and were building together. We in the university learned how the community felt about "poverty pimping" by outsiders; community residents learned that some outsiders could be trusted. This is an ongoing co-learning experience about each other as we struggle together against racism and poverty to build a community that nurtures rather than oppresses its residents. To date, the community has accomplished several goals: developed a computer resource center in their housing complex, operated a one-year computer-based program to increase their children's skills, established a women's literacy program, and begun a newsletter for the residents. Leadership is being learned, and residents are making history. And we have begun to understand what co-learning means.

Co-Learning as Constructing Knowledge in the Community

Teaching and learning are separated out from each other within formal education, the concepts often conflated with the concept of professionalism. This separation leads to role differentiation: teachers are experts who provide knowledge; students are learners or receivers of knowledge. These distinctions seem unnecessary to us as adult educators for three reasons: (1) they lead to the objectification of another adult, thereby creating asymmetrical power relations, which shapes the learning taking place; (2) they deny the experiential learning and the created knowledge of the adult learner, thus marginalizing their ideas; and (3) they deny the dialectical nature of the teaching-learning transaction.

Much of adult education is geared to the needs and goals of the individual learner. However, we recognize that learning is not solely an individual activity or a personal transformation for two reasons: learning is based on the cultural practices in which an individual finds meaning, and learning has both personal and social dimensions (Cunningham, 1998). Accordingly, learning, by our definition, is social in terms of its goals and its origins. Brookfield (1986) has argued that only to facilitate or animate learners' groups is to not accept one's responsibility as the teacher. Yet we believe that the case can be made that in social situations focusing on social learning, the responsibility belongs equally to all involved. After all, each has knowledge. Co-learning is one way to equalize power relationships and to deny socially constructed privilege or the privileging of one knowledge over another.

Many before us have seen the value of team teaching and student group learning; others have recognized the concern over power and its effect on learning (Freire, 1995; Giroux, 1992). By defining the team as inclusive of participants and acknowledging learners as educators, our practice of co-learning goes further when constructing knowledge in the community. We make our case by first exploring two concepts: knowledge and making meaning, and knowledge, community intellectuals, and struggle.

Knowledge and Making Meaning. We accept the view that knowledge is socially constructed and is central to human beings' attempting to make meaning out of the world they live in. Berger and Luckmann (1967) have given one of the best descriptions of how we socially construct our realities. Humans apprehend nature and give meaning to what they apprehend. This social construction of the meaning of the environment is internalized and then shapes a person's outlook as one continues to apprehend. Accordingly, our socially constructed meaning becomes an active part of what we see, as it is retrojected back on to the environment through our senses. Human beings make meaning, and then construct and pass on to others their perceived reality. Thus, every human has the potential to be an intellectual (Gramsci, 1971). Co-learning is a strategy to encourage us to do intellectual activity. We actualize our intellectual potential as knowledge makers, not simply as knowledge consumers.

In many formal teacher-learner transactions, we learn to consume the knowledge of the "expert," so designated because their knowledge is privileged by the dominant members of society; thus the basis for a knowledge-power relationship is built.

Gramsci (1971) recognized that each social class or group has constructed knowledge in the interests of their class. Thus, for example, the urban poor understand and create very different knowledges about gentrification than city planners do. While City Hall lures young, affluent professionals back into the city to "revitalize" neighborhoods, poor people resist gentrification because the "hoods" are the places where they have made meaning (Haymes, 1995), and this is their space. In fact, Haymes argues that this is where co-learning can flourish as a "pedagogy of place." Haymes's pedagogy of place relies on the relationship of meaning making by African Americans to the physical urban places where they reestablished their culture from the rural South. Only they, who did the cultural work, understand the meaning they project onto their place.

As co-learners applying this concept of pedagogy of place, we had to appreciate the significance of the symbols and meaning-making events such as the Bud Biliken parade, which is distinct to Chicago's South Side. Initiated by an African American prior to the 1960 civil rights era, it is a public demonstration of black culture, black music, black creativity, and black accomplishments. Accordingly, participating in the parade becomes a way of transmitting important cultural meanings to youth and affirming the black community, and involvement in it is also an important way to develop leadership among community members.

Apffel-Marglin (1998), in writing about mutual learning, also helps us to see the importance of co-learning by urging us to respect in a profound way how people collectively make meaning in their lives. As one group apprehends another, the participants should be in mutual learning with one another rather than appropriating the other's culture and knowledge. The lesson we take from this analysis is nonappropriation, that is, relinquishing the power of our official knowledge as university persons so that we do not set aside, devastate, or ignore the way a community has organized itself. Co-learning is respectful of the other's place and meaning making.

Knowledge, Community Intellectuals, and Struggle. Popular educators, who seek social as well as personal transformation as their educational goal, recognize that all persons are capable of being intellectuals, yet not all are intellectuals. Intellectuals have to be developed by performing intellectual activity. Participatory research, study circles, and cultural production are three ways of encouraging active intellectual participation of co-learners. Participatory research builds on the concept of praxis, where learning and doing come together through communitarian action. Study circles tend to equalize the position and the power of participants; they encourage active learning because of their participatory nature. In our study circles we used only curriculum that came from the group and served as a starter for dialogue. Cultural production encourages learners to express their ideas through popular theater, wall murals, puppets, music, and dance. Two aspects to the cultural dimension contribute to the intellectual activity of co-learners: (1) the idea that we often accept our own symbols, uncritically, and (2) that our cultural symbols provide a platform to explore understandings of one another. Beginning to explore and understand the meanings attached to symbol in a cross-cultural context can create new intellectual understandings, as well as further cultural production.

Another important dimension of co-learning and cultural production is common struggle. Eyerman and Jamison (1991) liken social struggle to "a process of social learning in which movement organizations act as structuring forces, opening a space in which creative interaction between individuals can take place" (p. 55). They see knowledge as the product of a series of social encounters within movements, between movements, and, even more important, between movements and their established opponents. This new knowledge created by the struggle can now be compared with existing knowledge or knowledges. Our group has co-learned, and as co-learners we have become knowledge producers. In addition, we believe, like Newman (1994), that there are enemies and we must define them. Our struggle has enemies. In our Chicago work, one intriguing "enemy" is the formal adult education state policy, delineated by the Illinois State Board of Education. The board has no category for funding nonformal learning, and so because we do not have teachers, students, and formal curriculum, we struggle to find funds to co-learn. Further, because these professionals appear to resist new ways of educating poor people, we interact with participatory literacy educators such as Fingeret (1989), gender educators such as Walters and Manicom (1996), and bottom-up community activists such as Foley (1999). We thus build a different way to frame our adult educational practice and attempt to persuade others. We see evolving a cognitive praxis that recaptures a tradition of friend teaching friend (Lindeman, 1926) and a growing body of practical knowledge that challenges "learning for earning," deficiency discourses, as well as professionalism and adult reproductive schooling.

The Distinctiveness of Co-Learning in Adult Education

A number of learning strategies may seem similar to co-learning. And although these other strategies have some of the same components as co-learning, they do not cover the entire definition of co-learning as we have experienced it.

First, we reject Knowles's (1980) notion of andragogy because it places the individual and self-directed learning at the center of the learning and relegates the collective to the periphery. Welton (1995) suggests in his critique of andragogy that as a guiding principle of the modern practice of adult education, self-directed learning is conceptually inadequate to serve the interests of the poor, oppressed, and disenfranchised because of its overemphasis on the individual. Co-learning, by contrast, puts the collective at the center of learning while also allowing for personal development. A common proverb among the poor is that "need is the motherhood of invention"; that is, those who are poor are constantly constructing ways to survive with the resources they have. This knowledge production created around survival issues is rarely done in a vacuum; it is usually done collectively.

Second, there are elements to co-learning that seem similar to collaborative learning. Lawrence (1996) notes in her research on collaborative learning in cohorts that there is an assumption that an educator (instructor) has the overriding responsibility to teach students to value their own experience and respect their own knowledge. Horton and Freire (1990) suggest that in this way, the instructor validates an individual's knowledge. The group members begin to see value in the knowledge of others as well as their own knowledge. But collaborative and cohort learning are usually done in a formal setting with structured outcomes. By contrast, co-learning is done in a nonformal setting without a leader who has the responsibility of validating the group's knowledge.

Co-learning in the community does have important parallels to Freire's (1995) emphasis on conscientization and consciousness raising. Like Freire's approach, co-learning emphasizes levels of increasing awareness for learners in perceiving social, political, and economic contradictions, and taking action against the oppressive elements of reality. Similarly, Foley (1999) notes that feminist scholarship, which burgeoned from the 1960s onward, provides a rich source of data on the development of women's political consciousness through participation in political struggle. He also points out that consciousness and learning are central to the process of cultural and social reproduction and transformation. However, neither Freire nor Foley appears to recognize the issues of double or triple consciousness—the effects of dealing with multiple systems of oppression, such as race *and* gender, *and/or* class—for many members of marginalized groups. This is an emphasis in co-learning. Particularly relevant to our work of co-learning on Chicago's South Side is an emphasis on Afrocentric knowing and spiritual learning.

Afrocentric Knowing. Shaw (1992) argues that African Americans have an Afrocentric way of knowing that could be characterized by learning with the whole mind, living the experience, and creating through transcendence. Rogers's (1999) study of twelve African American political leaders lends support to Shaw's assertion. Rogers found that the success of the leaders she studied was based on their ability to practice "Afrotics," which embodies the notion of having a holistic outlook on their community while dealing with everyday life. She points out that these women leaders' survival depended on keeping the whole of the people at the center, not on the margin. Our definition of co-learning is more in line with Shaw's and Rogers's assumption that knowledge is holistic.

bell hooks (1984), in describing what needed to be done to promote sisterhood, states, "Unless we can show that barriers separating women can be eliminated, that solidarity does exist, we cannot hope to change and transform society as a whole" (p. 44). She was referring to relationship building and reducing barriers between white women and women of color, precisely the kind of barriers that are recognized when we engage in a co-learning experience. We enter the community expecting that other co-learners will see us as activist scholars and as outsiders, particularly those of us who are European American. We transcend those barriers through developing trust in our everyday work together. We as activist scholars learn what is important to the community and what the ground rules are from which we will operate. They learn why we are in their community and what our intentions are. Once these facts are established, we can work together to build solidarity around issues of social justice.

Residents, in their struggle for basic needs, maintain a holistic approach to community life, which includes what Du Bois (1961) calls a double consciousness. Those who both live in poverty and are people of color must understand the political reality of the world that they live in. Shaw (1992) often refers to double consciousness as the way that African Americans learn. Collins (1990), Giddings (1984), hooks (1984), and Weems (1993) go further to say that there is a triple consciousness for African American women. They describe the third consciousness as being an African American woman in a patriarchal society. Co-learning means that you understand your own social location and are willing to respect the social location of others, for example, the double and triple consciousness of others' reality.

Spiritual Learning. Spirituality could also be characterized as a significant variable in co-learning. We are not suggesting one must be spiritual in order to co-learn. What we are saying is that there is a faith base and an acknowledgment of a power greater than oneself in the equation. For example, Baker-Houston (1991) describes African American intellectual history as preeminently occupied with nonmaterial transactions and spiritual workings. He argues for a theoretical return to an African American vernacular and characteristically autobiographical expression. The spirit work that Baker refers to throughout his book is centered on a faith-based belief system where happiness and success are not measured by material gain. Our experience has shown us that co-learning teaches you to see the leaders as the people see the leaders. Hurston (1978) in *Mules and Men* says it best:

> No one may approach the altar without the crown, and none may wear the crown of power without preparation. It must be earned. And what is this crown of power? Nothing definite in material, Turner crowned me with a consecrated snakeskin. I have been crowned in other places with flowers, with ornament paper, with cloth, with sycamore bark, with eggshells. It is the meaning, not the material that counts [p. 38].

Susan Taylor (1994) believes that intuition is a higher form of mind than rational thinking; it is a synthesis of the heart, mind, and soul. In her book on spirituality, she reminds us that throughout history, the people who have made a difference in the world have known that there is magic in believing. She reports that in 1792, Toussaint L'Ouverture led revolting enslaved Africans to freedom and created Haiti, the first free black nation. When Mary McLeod Bethune arrived in Daytona Beach, Florida, she was twenty-eight years old, a widowed mother with little money, and a big dream to build a school for black girls. "It is in my mind and in my soul," she often said. Madam J. Walker could neither read nor write, but she followed a vision that she believed was spiritually guided and became the first self-made female millionaire. Similarly, Rogers (1998) reports that the women leaders in her study "emphasized an internal motivation that was spiritual and based on their relationship with God. These factors may be more important than learning styles, curriculum models and technical rationality that characterize modern adult education" (p. xii). Lyn Hughes (unpublished interview, 1997) in historic North Pullman on the South Side of Chicago said, "Something would not let me just buy real estate and leave." She had to be active in improving the quality of life for those who lived there.

What we are saying is that the spirit that drove "the ancestors" to keep straight ahead and lifting as they climbed is embodied in the work on the South Side of Chicago. We regularly heard the phrases, "Something told me," or, "The spirit told me to do this." We as co-learners must respect this acknowledgment that there is spiritual power that guides our co-learners and that spirituality can be considered as one of the deeper ways of knowing.

Conclusion

We have tried in this chapter to define "team" in a unique way, as co-learning; we see co-learners as having a distinct understanding of knowledge. We refuse to privilege official knowledge; we do not want to allow formal roles (teacher-learner) that are rational extensions of asymmetrical power relationships in society to frame our learning.

We see nonformal education as central to bona-fide adult education. Education for us is not simply to reproduce existing power relationships, which so often occurs in formal education where institutional press, a privileged knowledge, and "keepers of the gate" shape learning. We struggle against reducing adult education to finding the most efficient and effective way to shape learners. In so doing, we become fixated on the learners and their problems, which we, as the knowers, will solve.

We take Scipio A. J. Colin III's challenge given to the professors of adult education over a decade ago: "Are we keepers of the gate or keepers of the dream?" (1990). Our goal is to encourage all of us in the field to challenge existing conventions and knowledge and to see struggle as "keepers of the dream."

We understand learning sites to be contested terrain. It is our position that struggle against asymmetrical power relationships can provide the tools for developing our critical intellectual capacity. Co-learning reminds us of our equality and provides a frame for developing mutual, nonappropriating learning from and with one another.

References

Apffel-Marglin, F., with PRATEC (eds.). *The Spirit of Regeneration: Andean Culture Confronting Western Notions of Development.* New York: Zed Books, 1998.

Baker-Houston, A. *Working of the Spirit: The Poetics of Afro-American Women's Writings.* Chicago: University of Chicago Press, 1991.

Berger, P., and Luckmann, T. *The Social Construction of Reality: A Treatise in the Sociology of Knowledge.* New York: Doubleday, 1967.

Brookfield, S. *Understanding and Facilitating Adult Learning.* San Francisco: Jossey-Bass, 1986.

Colin, S.A.J. III Keynote speech, Commissions of Professors of Adult Education, Salt Lake City, Utah, 1990.

Collins, P. H. *Black Feminist Thought.* New York: Routledge, 1990.

Cunningham, P. "The Social Dimension of Adult Education." *PACE Journal of Lifelong Learning,* 1998, 7, 15–28.

Du Bois, W.E.B. *The Souls of Black Folks.* Greenwich, Conn.: Fawcett, 1961.

Eyerman, R., and Jamison, A. *Social Movements: A Cognitive Approach.* University Park: Pennsylvania State University Press, 1991.

Fingeret, A. "The Social and Historical Context of Participatory Literacy Education." In A. Fingeret and P. Jurno (eds.), *Participatory Literacy Education.* San Francisco: Jossey-Bass, 1989.

Foley, G. *Learning in Social Action.* New York: Zed Books, 1999.

Freire, P. *Pedagogy of the Oppressed.* New York: Continuum, 1995.

Giddings, P. *When and Where I Enter.* New York: Bantam Books, 1984.

Giroux, H. *Border Crossing: Cultural Workers and the Politics of Education.* New York: Routledge, 1992.

Gramsci, A. *Selections from the Prison Notebooks.* New York: International Publishers, 1971.

Haymes, S. *Race, Culture and the City: A Pedagogy for Black Urban Struggle.* New York: State University of New York Press, 1995.

hooks, b. *From Margin to Center.* Boston: South End Press, 1984.

Horton, M., and Freire, P. *We Make the Road by Walking.* Philadelphia: Temple University Press, 1990.

Hurston, Z. N. *Mules and Men.* New York: HarperCollins, 1978.

Knowles, M. S. *The Modern Practice of Adult Education: From Pedagogy to Andragogy.* New York: Cambridge Books, 1980.

Lawrence, R. "Co-Learning Communities: A Hermeneutic Account of Adult Learning in Higher Education Through the Lived World of Cohorts." Unpublished doctoral dissertation, Northern Illinois University, 1996.

Lindeman, E. *The Meaning of Adult Education.* New York: New Republic, 1926.

Newman, M. *Defining the Enemy: Adult Education in Social Action.* Sydney: Stewart Victor Publishing, 1994.

Rogers, E. "An Ethnographic Case Study of Chicago African American Female Political Leaders." Unpublished doctoral dissertation, Northern Illinois University, 1998.

Rogers, E. "Afrotics." Paper presented at the African American preconference of the Adult Education Research Conference, Northern Illinois University, De Kalb, Ill., 1999.

Shaw, M. "African American Strategies of Successful Adaptation in Response to Diseducation: A Phenomenological Investigation." Unpublished doctoral dissertation, Northern Illinois University, 1992.

Taylor, S. *In the Spirit.* New York: HarperCollins, 1994.

Walters, S., and Manicom, L. (eds.). *Gender in Popular Education: Methods for Empowerment.* London: Zed Books, 1996.

Weems, C. *Africana Womanism: Reclaiming Ourselves.* Troy, N.Y.: Bedford Publishing, 1993.

Welton, M. *In Defense of the Life World.* Albany: State University of New York Press, 1995.

REGINA M. CURRY *is a scholar-activist and a doctoral candidate at Northern Illinois University.*

PHYLLIS CUNNINGHAM *is a scholar-activist and professor of adult education at Northern Illinois University.*

9

This chapter highlights three central themes of the other chapters in this volume as central to team teaching and learning: relationship development, task completion, and collaborative knowledge construction.

Team Teaching and Learning in Adult Education: From Negotiating Relationships to Implementing Learning Alternatives

Elizabeth J. Tisdell, Mary-Jane Eisen

It is the morning of April 15, 2000 (*tax day!*). In the midst of the busyness of our personal lives (mailing off our tax return and seeing to our children, parents, partners, friends, and pets), along with the ever present demands of our professional lives (grading papers, responding to student e-mails, doing our administrative work), we are trying to finish the editing on this book. We are also coauthoring this final chapter. We have come up with an outline of what it might look like and have sort of agreed on a plan of who is writing what. Still, each of us wonders, "Have I understood which part I'm supposed to be writing? Will we come from a similar perspective? What about our writing styles? Will they mesh? Do we use 'I' language when we are talking about one of us in particular, or do we refer to ourselves in the third person, or use 'we' language? Will our feedback on each other's writing seem too harsh? What about our e-mail difficulty with sending attachments? Will this be a hassle in writing this chapter and finishing up this project, now in its final stages?" Indeed, this is reality. Editing a book, writing a chapter, team-teaching a class, teaming up with another to work on any project that has a product attached to it is essentially about two things: negotiating relationships and completing the task.

We begin with this short vignette, capturing some of our process of working together, because we think it has a familiar ring to it. The process of team teaching and learning, including coauthoring and coediting as a team teaching—learning endeavor, means both attending to the task itself

NEW DIRECTIONS FOR ADULT AND CONTINUING EDUCATION, no. 87, Fall 2000   © Jossey-Bass

and attending to the relationship between collaborators in the process. Indeed, the literature in adult education, both that written by the chapter authors in this book as well as others (Foley, 1992; Saltiel, Sgroi, and Brockett, 1999), corroborates the importance of balancing the relationship needs of team members with the goal of getting the job done. A third theme would be the excitement of creating new knowledge together. Thus, in concluding this volume on team teaching and learning, we highlight the relational and task completion and implementation challenges inherent in teaming, as well as the underlying significance of creating collaborative forms of knowledge.

Negotiating Relationships

All who engage in team teaching and learning or collaborative work of any other kind must attend on some level to the relationship among collaborators. This is an ongoing process, which usually causes teammates (for good, or for ill) to get to know each other much better. Sometimes team members know each other well when they begin a project; other times they have never met. Some collaborators share a lot about the overlap of their personal lives in the process; others share very little.

We barely knew each other when we first met over breakfast at a conference to discuss teaming up to coedit this volume. Mary-Jane was familiar with some of Libby's earlier writing, and Libby recognized Mary-Jane from other conferences. Yet it was our mutual interest in the topic of team teaching and learning that initially brought us together; thus, the task of working on the project was the driving force in our relationship at that point. As we got to know each other, the common threads we discovered in our professional interests and personalities reassured us that our partnership would work, and by the end of our first breakfast, we agreed to go forward. In addition to our common experience of team teaching in higher education, we found that our backgrounds were also complementary. Mary-Jane's experience with adult education in workplace settings and with older adults was balanced by Libby's emphasis in addressing diversity and equity issues and education for social action. We also sensed a compatibility in our personal styles, though it was not until later that we learned we share the same Myers-Briggs Type Indicator profile (Kroeger and Thuesen, 1988). All in all, we recognized that we had enough in common to feel comfortable together, but we were different enough to make the partnership interesting.

For us, the task of editing this volume—our actual work together—was primary, yet perhaps because we are women who fit Belenky, Clinchy, Goldberger, and Tarule's (1986) conception of "connected knowers," we are both extremely relationally oriented as well. Thus, even in the first six months of our relationship, when we communicated only by telephone and e-mail, our personal relationship grew as we attended to the editorial work we shared.

We learned a lot about each other's personal lives in side conversations about our day-to-day living and the life events that happened along the way—things that undeniably affected our book editing process. We saw Mary-Jane through her dissertation and dealt with Libby's grief and the significant spiritual experience of being present at her mother's death. A few months later, we decided to room together at a conference, primarily to work on our project but also to get to know each other better. In this context, we spontaneously shared some of our heritage and life stories. For instance, we discussed Libby's experience of growing up Irish-Catholic and of being a feminist who worked for the Catholic church for ten years, and Mary-Jane's background as a Jewish New Yorker who was born in Luxembourg, left there at the age of one and a half, and then returned with her husband and children just last summer. We have discussed career options, academia, dealing with aging parents, and our love lives.

On one level, the sharing of our personal lives may seem tangential to our work as editors, which entailed giving feedback to chapter authors and to each other, dividing tasks equitably, and accommodating to each other's strengths, weaknesses, timetables, and personal life. However, we believe that our ability to accomplish the overall task of finishing this book with relatively little conflict is due to the fact that we have attended to both relational and task issues either right from the beginning or as they arose along the way. In so doing, we developed a high degree of trust in each other, which laid the groundwork for us to give and receive authentic and constructive criticism. These reciprocal critiques became a source of professional development for each of us.

Thus, given the significance we both place on relationship, the personal aspects of our partnership were integral to our satisfaction with the process we shared and the product we co-produced. We are proud that we completed this book and acknowledge that it is the pleasure of our personal relationship that made the project fun. Admittedly, other collaborators might not place as much emphasis on their relationship or the sharing of their personal lives, and they may derive more satisfaction from completing the task itself, but for us, our relationship is as important as the task.

Not all of the chapter authors discussed the personal dimensions of their relationship as directly as we do here, yet, to be sure, they allude to the importance of negotiating relationships in order to accomplish their team teaching and learning objectives. For example, in Chapter One, Mary-Jane identifies a typology of teaching-learning teams that is based principally on how team members interrelate. Represented in her typology are teams of teachers who develop very interdependent relationships that lead to blended presentation formats, teams comprising highly autonomous players who tend to function serially or in parallel, and teams that are unusually inclusive, to the extent that they involve learners and teachers in close partnership with each other.

Marcia Seabury and Karen Barrett, directors of a team-taught, interdisciplinary program for undergraduates, come at the relational dimension of teaming from an administrative perspective. In Chapter Two, they echo Mary-Jane's position that members of different teams have variable preferences, and they suggest giving team members the freedom to work together accordingly, since a one-size-fits-all approach is not usually optimally productive. Candace Harris and Anne Harvey, in Chapter Three, take a different tack, specifically referencing their own dyadic partnership. They demonstrate how their mutual trust allowed them to play off each other and take risks in the classroom that they might not have taken in the absence of such a supportive working relationship. Similarly, in Chapter Four, Gabriele Strohschen and Tom Heaney emphasize that the camaraderie they established in their dyad supported their entry into the new terrain of online education, a challenge that would have been far more daunting if they had faced it alone.

One focus of Chapter Five, by Judy O'Neil and Sharon Lamm, is on building effective relationships among teammates, who happen to be action learning coaches, by helping them to appreciate diversity and practice reciprocal coaching. The relationships among the coaches then becomes a model of sorts for the kind of respect that each of these coaches is expected to foster in his or her respective action learning group. In Chapter Six, D. Todd Evans and Jane Hugo stress the need to help members of literacy volunteer certification teams negotiate conflict and divide up tasks appropriately so that relationships support goal achievement. Viviana Aguilar and Ginlin Woo in Chapter Seven highlight the significance of relationship in their culturally diverse facilitation team, and of allowing for check-in times during planning meetings as central to creating the climate necessary for authentic dialogue around diversity issues. Finally in Chapter Eight, explicitly defining team members as co-learners from the community, Regina Curry and Phyllis Cunningham emphasize the need to negotiate relationships between and among university workers and community members in order to construct knowledge collaboratively, develop mutual respect, and create projects and events that meet neighborhood needs.

Notably, strong teaching-learning teams are not conflict free (Eisen, 1999). Rather, their members build relationships that are resilient enough to work through conflict to improve their functioning by allowing diverse ideas to be heard and by finding ways to integrate new ideas into thoughtful action that benefits both the team members and the target learners alike.

It seems that a foundation of trust and respect is integral to productive teamwork. That is, members of the most successful team efforts are able to build enough trust to negotiate fairly the tasks that need to be accomplished, to learn to compromise, and to give and receive authentic feedback that is reciprocal and formative, not unidirectional or punitive. Not everyone develops a personal friendship in the process; however, successful teaming definitely requires attending to relationships.

Attending to the Task

More often than not, the impetus for people to team up in adult education is rooted in an educational task, such as planning and teaching a class. As Mary-Jane notes in Chapter One, there are at least eight types of teams that can be differentiated according to their defining goals or tasks: providing interdisciplinary and/or multicultural education; fostering collaborative learning; effecting community action and co-learning; facilitating action learning; providing specialized education or delivering it in an innovative way; developing the team members professionally; conducting research; and writing a book such as this one. Whether a team has a unitary goal or multiple goals, success requires the completion of many tasks. Teamwork creates possibilities for lightening the load by dividing up responsibilities, enlivening otherwise tedious tasks through camaraderie, increasing confidence about task completion by providing moral support, and enhancing task performance by piggybacking on each other's strengths and creativity. On the downside, teaming can slow progress at times, while time is consumed understanding and negotiating work style differences among teammates. (This brings us full circle to our earlier discussion of the relational side of teaming.)

All of the chapter authors examined the task orientation of their respective teaching-learning teams. For instance, Seabury and Barrett provide numerous tips for administrators of team-taught interdisciplinary programs on how to achieve the overarching task of not only keeping such an initiative going but keeping it fresh. Harris and Harvey describe their methods for helping students in their "Art of Learning" class become more critically reflective and more confident in their ability to create new knowledge together. Strohschen and Heaney's efforts vivify the task of teaching in cyberspace and creating a sense of community among learners in the absence of face-to-face gatherings.

Evans and Hugo report on how they implemented their task, which entailed decentralizing a national literacy training and certification process to meet increasingly divergent local needs, while instituting team accountability for adherence to standards of professionalism. O'Neil and Lamm are explicit about the challenge of attending to completing the task that their client, a recently deregulated public utility, hired them to do. Their action-oriented action learning program design has the dual focus of facilitating their participants' learning while also delivering innovative strategies for ensuring organizational success in a new business climate.

Aguilar and Woo help service volunteers become more sensitive to diversity issues of all types. They do this by attention to climate setting, exploring how systems of privilege and oppression work with participants in their lives and in their communities, and having a strong commitment to neither whitewash diversity issues nor alienate participants in the process. Curry and Cunningham have also stood firm in their commitment of co-learning in the community, constructing new knowledge in the community as they work on projects together, such as the Bud Biliken parade and the new film about the A. Phillip Randolph museum. At the same time, they developed an understanding of the "pedagogy of place" and an even greater sense of symbolic meaning as they experienced the collaborative process in action.

The Construction of New Knowledge

The very purpose of adult education and learning, and of team teaching and learning, is for teachers and learners to be engaged in the process of constructing new knowledge. The key in team teaching and learning is that participants do it together. We contend that the process of new knowledge construction is a direct result of the effective interplay between the task and relationship functions, as collaborators play off each other and forge a productive dialogic interplay together. Just as the chapters in this volume illustrate the interplay between task achievement and relationship building, they also demonstrate the energy generated when people come together to make meaning, whether in an academic setting, a workplace, a volunteer training effort, or a community action initiative.

Our educational landscape has changed dramatically over the past century and will most certainly continue to transform in response to ever-shifting global trends in information production, technology, work, leisure, and a host of other arenas. The resulting explosion of demand for and options in adult education necessitates the use of alternative teaching modalities that are optimally inclusive and learner focused. Team teaching and learning is one such modality. Although its potential has been realized in many contexts already, as illustrated by the writing teams who contributed to this volume, much more promise lies ahead. We leave the challenge of tapping this gold mine of opportunity for adult learning by exploring team teaching and learning applications in your own unique practice setting.

References

Belenky, M., Clinchy, B., Goldberger, N., and Tarule, J. *Women's Ways of Knowing*. New York: Basic Books, 1986.
Eisen, M. J. "Peer Learning Partnerships: A Qualitative Case Study of Teaching Partners' Professional Development Efforts." Unpublished doctoral dissertation, Teachers College, Columbia University, 1999.
Foley, G. "Going Deeper: Teaching and Group Work in Adult Education." *Studies in the Education of Adults*, 1992, 24(2), 143–161.
Kroeger, O., and Thuesen, J. M. *Type Talk: The 16 Personality Types That Determine How We Live, Love, and Work*. New York: Dell, 1988.
Saltiel, I. M., Sgroi, A., and Brockett, R. G. (eds.). *The Power and Potential of Collaborative Learning Partnerships*. New Directions for Adult and Continuing Education, no. 79. San Francisco: Jossey-Bass, 1999.

ELIZABETH J. TISDELL is associate professor in the Department of Adult and Continuing Education at National-Louis University in Chicago.

MARY-JANE EISEN is director, workforce development, for the Connecticut Technology Council and adjunct faculty at the University of Hartford, Saint Joseph's College, and American International College.

INDEX

Back Issue/Subscription Order Form

Copy or detach and send to:
Jossey-Bass, 350 Sansome Street, San Francisco CA 94104-1342

Call or fax toll free!
Phone 888-378-2537 6AM-5PM PST; Fax 800-605-2665

Back issues: Please send me the following issues at $23 each.
(Important: please include series initials and issue number, such as ACE78.)

1. ACE _____

_____

_____

$ _____ Total for single issues

$ _____ Shipping charges (for single issues *only;* subscriptions are exempt
from shipping charges): Up to $30, add $5^{50} • $30^{01}–$50, add $6^{50}
$50^{01}–$75, add $8 • $75^{01}–$100, add $10 • $100^{01}–$150, add $12
Over $150, call for shipping charge.

Subscriptions   Please ❑ start   ❑ renew my subscription to *New Directions
for Adult and Continuing Education* for the year _____ at the
following rate:

U.S.:	❑ Individual $58	❑ Institutional $104
Canada:	❑ Individual $83	❑ Institutional $129
All Others:	❑ Individual $88	❑ Institutional $134

NOTE: Subscriptions are quarterly, and are for the calendar year only.
Subscriptions begin with the Spring issue of the year indicated above.

$ _____ Total single issues and subscriptions (Add appropriate sales tax for
your state for single issues. No sales tax on U.S. subscriptions. Canadian
residents, add GST for subscriptions and single issues.)

❑ Payment enclosed (U.S. check or money order only)

❑ VISA, MC, AmEx, Discover Card # _____ Exp. date_____

Signature _____ Day phone _____

❑ Bill me (U.S. institutional orders only. Purchase order required.)

Purchase order #_____

Federal Tax I.D. 135593032   GST 89102-8052

Name _____

Address _____

_____

Phone_____ E-mail _____

For more information about Jossey-Bass, visit our Web site at:
www.josseybass.com   **PRIORITY CODE = ND1**